HIGH COUNTRY STATIONS OF THE
MACKENZIE

HIGH COUNTRY STATIONS OF THE
MACKENZIE

MARY HOBBS

pb potton & burton

First published in 2015 by Potton & Burton

Potton & Burton
98 Vickerman Street, PO Box 5128, Nelson, New Zealand
pottonandburton.co.nz

© Mary Hobbs

ISBN 978 1 927213 51 3

Printed in China by Midas Printing International Ltd

CONTENTS

Lenticular clouds over Lake Pukaki and the Ben Ohau Range. MARY HOBBS

ACKNOWLEDGEMENTS

Telling the stories of the early days in the Mackenzie was only possible because the early settlers had the foresight to write fascinating accounts of their lives for future generations to enjoy. It was wonderful to be able to read their stories. They felt like old friends by the time I had finished writing this book. Thank you to all of these wonderful characters.

I am very grateful for the assistance from current and past station owners who provided me with genuine, warm hospitality, and kindly shared stories of their lives and the history of their stations. A big thank you to Simon and Priscilla Cameron of Ben Ohau, who willingly gave me a wealth of information and also permission to use Brian Barry's outstanding poem and Jane Stronach's memoir. A special thank you to Linda Hayman and her son Ian for their warm hospitality and welcome at Tasman Downs Station; to Ian's wife Nicky for ensuring I received corrections to the story on time, and also to Robert, who guards Tasman Downs with a sharp eye and provided much hilarity.

Thank you to Gillian and Justin Wills of Irishman Creek for their enthusiasm, and lending me some fine reference material. Grateful thanks to Caro Murray for telling me many stories of Braemar Station and The Wolds and being so generous with her time. Many thanks also to John and Bronwen Murray for helping me get the facts right. Thank you to Duncan and Carol Mackenzie and also Julia and Mish Mackenzie for their kindness and showing me parts of their magnificent Braemar Station.

Thank you to Denis Fastier and his partner Jane Stevenson, and Sarah and Glenn Fastier, for their warm hospitality, and for taking me out to that old orchard more than once! Thank you also to Mrs Hosken's daughter Evelyn Middlemiss and her daughter Raewyn Atkinson for their time and generous permission to retell many of Mrs Hosken's wonderful old stories. A warm thank you to Gilbert and Marion Seymour of Ferintosh Station for their wide knowledge of the history of the Mackenzie and being available to share it, along with some precious pages from Bill Seymour's journal. Thank you to Jim and Anne Murray, formerly of Glenmore Station, for their assistance and for permission to use the photos of George and Mary Murray. Thank you also to Mark and Kate Ivey of Glentanner.

Thank you to Diana Rhodes, the daughter of photographer Havelock Williams, for her generous permission to use photos from her father's outstanding collection. I was very appreciative of the assistance of Mike Hamilton, Bill and Peggy Hamilton's grandson, Chairman of the Board of Directors of Hamilton Jet, who was very helpful in terms of checking the Irishman Creek story and his assistance in providing images. Thank you to Jack Adamson's grandson Pat for the kind use of some of his grandfather's photos.

I was also very appreciative of the generous assistance of Maureen and Michael Vance who kindly clarified information and gave permission to refer to their father, William Vance's fine book in the text. Thank you also to Maureen and Ray Binnie for their reminisces.

Thank you to Olwyn Whitehouse for providing online source references, and to Lynley Eade for her foresight in interviewing and preserving stories of the older farmers in the district for her publication, *Twizel Town and Around*.

In the event that I may have omitted naming anyone who has been helpful, I do apologise in advance. Please accept my grateful thanks.

An immense thank you to the great team at Potton & Burton, particularly Robbie Burton, who was a delight to work with and ensured the author was always part of the process, which made it that much more special. Thank you also to talented designer Victoria Wigzell for her input, and to my literary agent Vicki Marsdon. A huge thank you to my close friends and wonderful family, particularly my husband Charlie, who, as always, was there for the duration.

—MH

INTRODUCTION

This book contains a range of stories, both old and new, of inspirational people on high country stations who call the Mackenzie Country home. The original intention was to cover most stations in the area, but it quickly became apparent that this was an impossible task, because there were just too many great tales to tell. So, this volume is limited to most of the stations that surround Lake Pukaki and lead up to the Southern Alps and Aoraki/Mt Cook.

Once over Burkes Pass, the landscape dramatically opens out to the immense space of the Mackenzie Country, a vast, golden tussock-covered basin that stretches back to impressive snow-capped mountains in the distance, beneath endless skies that change in mood and hue as often as the weather. Lakes of aquamarine and turquoise, fed by glacial rivers, provide dramatic contrast, while towering over this landscape is Aoraki/Mt Cook, the highest mountain in New Zealand.

Days can dawn with the most innocent shade of palest pink, as mountains softly reflect their image in calm, still lakes, before giving way to scorching, cloudless summer days. A deceptively small breeze may then spring up and, before long, clouds form and billow and a nor'wester strengthens to gale-force, accompanied by torrential rain. Thunder rumbles amongst the mountains, as forks of lightening ignite the sky. Yet, the next day may dawn bright and sunny, and stay that way for weeks. That is all part of the thrill of living in the Mackenzie.

I've lived on the edge of the Mackenzie, up from the head of Lake Pukaki, at Aoraki/Mount Cook Village, with my husband, a mountain guide, for decades. I have sworn over it while clearing metres of snow from the front door in a heavy winter, revelled in the climbing, skiing and alpine trekking, frozen in mountain huts, and been kept awake at night by spectacular storms that have almost shaken our home from its foundations. Yet, I have also been brought to tears by the indescribable beauty

Lake Pukaki and Aoraki/Mt Cook, early morning. MARY HOBBS

of the sunrises and sunsets over the Southern Alps and Lake Pukaki, as the sky turns from aquamarine to delicate shades of blue, pink and indigo and the tussock melds into a carpet of shimmering gold. It wasn't long before this uncompromising and beautiful landscape touched me deeply, and became home.

At first glance, it may well look as though this barren land, named after James Mackenzie, a Highland sheep rustler of the 1800s who is credited with being the first white person to find a pass into it, has little in the way of history or stories. Nothing could be further from the truth. Each stream, almost every corner in the road, and every high country station, holds rich stories of those who have made their homes here and left their imprint upon this land.

I have always been very curious about the stories behind those iconic mailboxes in the Mackenzie. Who lives there and how have they fared? Who were the first settlers and what tales of them lay hidden in this land? The answers to many of those questions became this book.

Some of the old stories illustrate the struggles of the first settlers. Others retell tales in danger of being lost. The historical accounts are combined with contemporary stories that offer the reader a glimpse of the challenges and joys of high country life in an area that has fascinated New Zealanders for many years. They include poignant accounts of tragedy and hardship, yet there are also stories of friendship, reward, and laughter, but whatever emotion they evoke, they won't fail to inspire.

Many of the first settlers were from the Scottish Highlands, where the terrain, the weather, and shepherding in lonely, remote locations were all familiar conditions. Over the years since, the people who have settled here have come from a wide variety of fascinating backgrounds. A traveller journeying through the Mackenzie today, will pass the home of the inventor of the world-famous jet boat; a pilot from the Second World War; winners of international awards for top merino fleece; a Rough Rider from the Boer War who later lost an arm when attacked by a tiger in India; international award-winning glider pilots; inventors; mountain guides; writers; poets and artists.

What is it that draws such people to this land and makes them persevere in the extremes of scorching hot summers and cold, snowy winters where neighbours are few? Helen Wilson wrote in her book, *My First Eighty Years*, that those who lived here 'always spoke and acted as if belonging to the Mackenzie Country added cubits to their stature.' Yet, as station owner Simon Cameron said, 'Perhaps it does, as those who live amongst these mountains or on these stations are constantly battling the elements and many who endure it have earned the badge of perseverance, and stand a little taller, as a result'.

The isolation here is more than compensated for by an unspoken and strong relationship with the environment. A long walk in this country offers invaluable gifts from nature, solves problems, and inspires great ideas. It doesn't matter what the weather is doing, there is always something magnificent about the view and the space.

High country station owners are not necessarily known for saying much about such matters but, in a rare moment, in a poem, or perhaps a few words, one may hear of their depth of feeling for this country. John Murray describes it well:

> It is immense. The light changes as it reflects on the hills and the view is different every day. When it snows, and we're up before dawn to feed out, we're also in time to see the sun set the world of white alight with crystals that dance on the snow like countless millions of sparkling diamonds. It is a constantly changing land of contrast with the way the light reflects on the land, where different cloud formations forecast the weather. In these moments it is a land like no other.

After a while, the space envelops those living here and offers a sense of belonging. It is a place that is carried in the heart. From the summit of Aoraki/Mt Cook, to the rivers, the aquamarine lakes and the golden rolling tussock, where the light casts a splendour on the landscape every day – it is a place we call home.

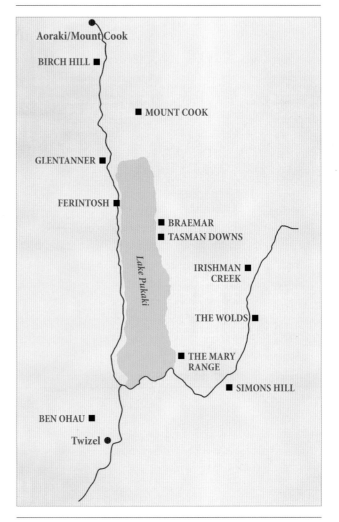

The approximate locations of the high country stations featured in this book. Note that Birch Hill and The Mary Range no longer exist.

OPPOSITE An early map from 1889 showing Pastoral Runs around Lake Pukaki.
CAMERON FAMILY COLLECTION

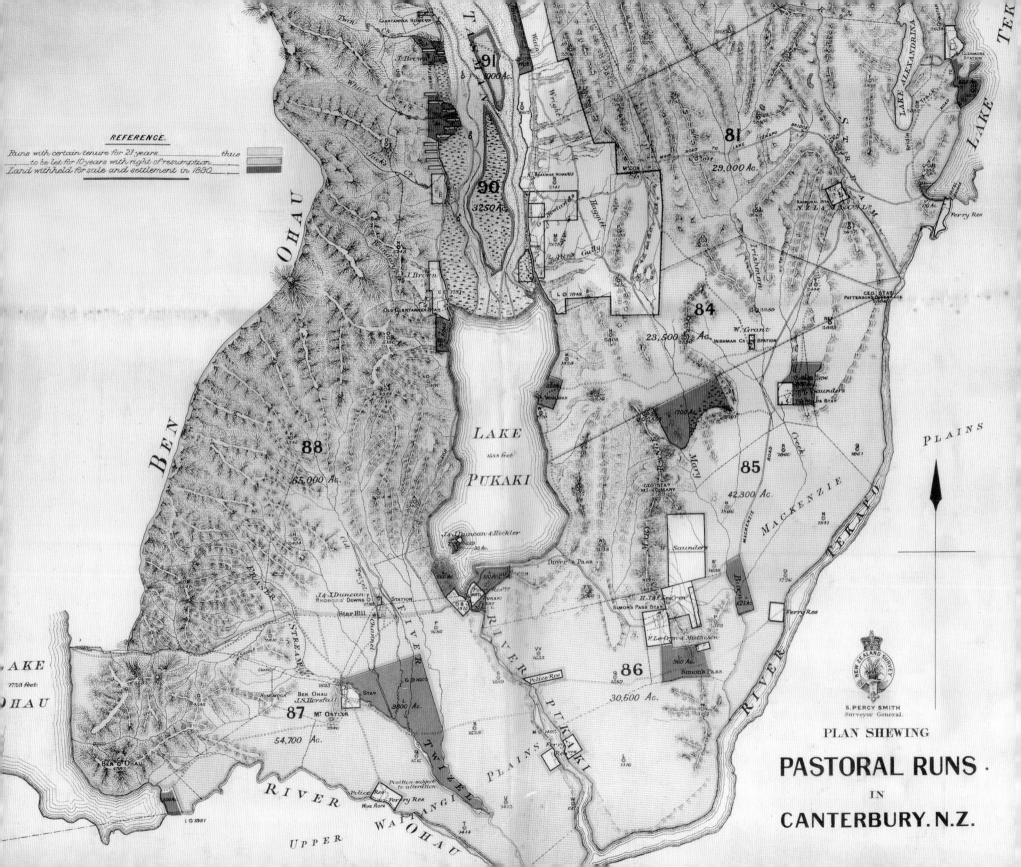

REFERENCE.

Runs with certain tenure for 21 years _____ thus
to be let for 10 years with right of resumption _____
Land withheld for sale and settlement in 1890 _____

OHAU

BEN

LAKE OHAU
1723 feet

AKE OHAU

91
1000 Ac.

90
3250 Ac.

81
29,000 Ac.

84
23,500 Ac.

88
65,000 Ac.

85
42,300 Ac.

LAKE
1588 feet
PUKAKI

MACKENZIE

TEKAPO RIVER

PLAINS

86
30,600 Ac.

87
54,700 Ac.

Simon's Pass

TWIZEL STREAM

RIVER PUKAKI

PUKAKI PLAINS

RIVER WAITANGI OHAU

UPPER WAITANGI OHAU

NEW ZEALAND SURVEY

S. PERCY SMITH
Surveyor General.

PLAN SHEWING

PASTORAL RUNS

IN

CANTERBURY. N.Z.

THE MARY RANGE

In the early months of 1890, an elderly man, John McHutcheson, and his nephew, William McHutcheson, were two of thousands of visitors to see the New Zealand and South Seas Exhibition, held in Dunedin from November 1889 to April 1890. They were wandering through the Early History section when John came to an abrupt halt in front of an impressive oil painting by Nicholas Chevalier.[1] The spectacular scene of Aoraki/Mt Cook, with the aquamarine shades of Lake Pukaki in the foreground, revived many half-forgotten memories. William, impressed by the older man's enthusiasm, persuaded him to tell all he knew of this remote and mystical part of New Zealand.

William, amazed to discover that his uncle and aunt had been the first couple to establish a home in the Mackenzie Country, considered the stories worthy of publication in the *Otago Witness*. Under the general heading, 'The New Zealander at Home', William McHutcheson, who had already penned a series called 'The New Zealander Abroad', told his uncle's story in the first person, in a rollicking and lively style. 'Fifty Years of Colonial Life; or, The Story of a Jubilee Colonist' ran in the paper in 12 episodes from 14 August to 30 October 1890.[2]

Along with almost 200 other Highland Scots, John sailed from Scotland aboard the *Blenheim* and arrived in Wellington on 27 December 1840. He travelled with his sister, Eliza, her husband, Captain Francis

Lake Pukaki and Aoraki/Mt Cook in the late evening light, from near the McHutcheson's home. MARY HOBBS

Sinclair, and their six children – three sons and three daughters. According to William's account, he 'picked up sufficient Gaelic on the voyage out … to pose as a Highlander ever since'.

There was no housing available when they arrived so they built a simple whare made of toetoe in a small settlement originally known as Britannia and later renamed Petone. The newly arrived settlers 'lost no time in setting to work', which included helping to reap the first crop of wheat grown in the Hutt. With two others, John purchased a boat and built up a successful business ferrying timber to Wellington for the building of the future city and bringing provisions back to the Hutt. There was no jetty at Lambton Quay, so they had to take the cargo off the boat by wading ashore through breaking surf, while carrying the timber to where it was deposited above the high-water mark. On one occasion, their boat was swamped and they struggled in the water for several hours.

John managed to survive this, along with a later incident in which he was swept overboard.

After deciding to try farming in the Wanganui area, and travelling there in an 8-metre whaleboat they built themselves, John and his family and others found, to their great disappointment, that 'no land could be obtained with any certainty of tenure or boundaries' and land orders they had bought in London could not be filled. After some close and interesting encounters with local Maori, the group returned to Wellington and set about building another boat, the schooner *Richmond*, which was launched on 11 August 1842.[3] John and his brother-in-law put the vessel to good use trading and exploring around the coasts of both islands, and purchasing potatoes from the Maori at Moeraki and then selling them back in Wellington.

The pair were commissioned by a number of New Zealand Company landholders 'to report on the various parts of the South Island suitable for settlement'. John and his companions favoured Port Cooper (now known as Lyttelton) with the plains beyond. The Deans brothers, William and John, from Scotland, Ebenezer Hay and his family, and the McHutcheson and Sinclair families 'agreed to go down to Canterbury, and settle there'.

Captain Sinclair and John McHutcheson transported the Deans brothers, along with two other families who originally came out with them, the Gebbies and the Mansons, on 10 February 1843.[4] They arrived at Port Cooper, where several Maori in a whaleboat then ferried the Deans around to the Canterbury Plains. The Deans travelled up the Avon River as far as possible and pitched their camp near a 'small clump of bush' now known as Riccarton, where they decided to make their home.

The next shipload of citizens from Wellington in April included their own party, as well as the Hay family, along with 'two milch cows, a few goats and some domestic fowls'. They sailed around the immediate area until finally deciding to settle at Pigeon Bay, 'which at that time was in a state of undisturbed repose, and about as charming a spot as the heart of man could well desire'. After swapping their schooner for 20 head of cattle, they built yet another boat, the *Sisters*, on which they traded, bringing butter and cheese to Wellington.

In John's opinion, the Wairau 'massacre', as it was then known, near Blenheim in 1843, in which 22 Europeans and six Maori were killed, 'greatly emboldened the natives in all parts of the colony'. There was talk

among local Maori of 'sweeping the pakeha into the sea', so the early settlers had to remain vigilant. Stockades were built in Akaroa, valuables were hidden in the nearby bush, houses were barricaded and guns were kept loaded. The Port Levy Maori were apparently planning to kill all Europeans on the peninsula, starting at Pigeon Bay. Riccarton was also to be attacked. Since John's 'own particular little slab hut was the outermost outpost of civilisation by some miles', he would be first in line. Luckily it all came to nothing when 'an old chief with considerable influence' strongly urged that the campaign be abandoned. But other dangers were very real: Captain Sinclair and his eldest son George were drowned off the Kaikoura Coast, and not long afterwards William Deans lost his life in a shipwreck.

In 1845, John decided to return to Scotland for a visit, with three or four months in America en route. He became involved with the Otago Association, a group formed to assist early pioneers to emigrate from Scotland to Otago, opening an office in Glasgow. John watched the sailings of the first two pioneer ships of the Otago settlement, the *John Wickliffe* and the *Philip Laing*. He planned to follow soon afterwards, but contracted cholera and could not sail for fear of infecting others on board. He worked for his brother James, in Glasgow, then set up on his own account, but 'the colonial instincts were all too strong' and he 'could not settle down contentedly'. He returned to New Zealand, landing in Nelson in 1852.

John eventually worked his way back down to Pigeon Bay where he stayed for a further two years, but life for him was becoming 'altogether too comfortable and easy for ambitious youth'. The Canterbury Pilgrims had arrived on the First Four Ships and, in his view, the 'encroaching civilization was fast rounding off all the rougher corners of pioneer life'.

In 1854 John sailed from Lyttelton to Wellington, with the intention of going to Australia, but was persuaded by an old friend to help establish a branch of the Union Bank in Nelson. John, however, still yearned for the 'freedom of the hills'. Office confinement did not suit his adventurous disposition and, had it not been for the 'bewitchment of a certain pair of dark eyes, the bank would have been simply insufferable'.

The dark eyes belonged to Mary Gorrie and the couple were married in Nelson in 1856. They settled in Pigeon Bay, where they welcomed frequent visitors, including Governor George Grey and several of the founding fathers of Canterbury, such as John Robert Godley, James Edward FitzGerald and William Sefton Moorhouse. However, John still had his heart set on obtaining 'more elbow room' and with his nephew, Francis Sinclair, they made plans to venture into South Canterbury and North Otago to look for further tracts of uninhabited land.

With a young Maori, and a spare horse, they set off, only to discover that much of the best country had already been claimed. When they reached Moeraki, John returned home, but Francis undertook to go further inland and explore the Mackenzie Country. 'Following up the tributaries of the Waitaki … to Lakes Pukaki and Tekapo, he finally put in his pegs on the shore of the former, and came home full of its praises, and with glowing accounts of the wild grandeur of its sublime scenery.' John had reservations, however. Frank, as he called him,

was, and is, a poet, and of course this was all very well in its way
but as a practical grazier and retired banker fresh from overdrafts

and dishonoured station cheques, I had some doubts as to value of scenery for winter feed – some misgivings as to the pecuniary results of wintering cattle thereon, was dubious in fact whether or no we could really induce our stock to fatten themselves to any great extent on the sublime sights which Pukaki and Mount Cook were said to afford. [There was, though] nothing in the world like trying, so we fixed to take up a slice of the Mackenzie Country, and proceeded with our arrangements.

At the Land Office in Christchurch they secured their run of between 20,000 and 30,000 acres (8000 to 12,000 hectares) for 21 years at a farthing for the first seven years, a halfpenny for the next seven years and three farthings for the last seven years. They also purchased a small 30-acre (12-hectare) island on Lake Pukaki, which boasted 'the only decent bit of timber in the country', for the 'exquisitely absurd' price of £60 – £2 an acre. They were incensed that the Australians who came to New Zealand were sold land in the wilderness for only 5 to 10 shillings an acre.

It was 1856 when John and Mary set out with their business partners – John's nephew, Francis Sinclair, and Henry Gladstone, a cousin of the British prime minister, and two young part-Maori men. Wheeled transport was a luxury, as were horses, except for riding, so John and Francis built a large wooden sledge with iron runners to tow their provisions along the beach coastline with the assistance of bullocks. They also carried a 5-metre Maori canoe for crossing rivers. Then the travellers

yoked up our four staunch bullocks, saddled our three horses, whistled up our faithful 'collies' … and journeyed forth into the wilderness full of hope and energy, and as light-hearted and merry as a parcel of school-boys …We were, all of us, in our prime, and in the best of health and spirits. We were journeying forth into an unknown land certainly, but what of that! It only gave a zest to the journey. The whole country lay before us waiting to be subdued, and in the buoyancy of spirit we felt quite able to subdue it, and still have something left in hand. To me, only a month or two married, the whole thing was part and parcel of my honeymoon and enjoyed as such. To my wife's young and romantic fancy the trip was but an extended picnic, while Francis was a born explorer, never happy off horseback or comfortable sleeping elsewhere than under a tent or the shadow of a cabbage tree.

They found the Rakaia, Ashburton, Rangitata and other big rivers all bank-to-bank in flood. Undaunted, they unloaded the sledge, swam the horses and bullocks across, and then ferried themselves and their provisions over with their canoe. They quickly realised they had to jump out of the canoe, often with water up to their chests, in order to land it on the other side. After a 17-day haul, they finally reached Timaru, which at that time consisted of an accommodation house and some sheds. They received a warm welcome from George Rhodes and his family at the Levels Station and spent a few days resting there before making their way to Mackenzie Pass, where they stayed a night. Late the next evening they eventually crossed the Tekapo River and 'pitched our pioneer tents on the shores of Pukaki and proceeded to unfurl our banners to the evening breeze. Our banners were two pairs of pants, accidentally soaked in crossing the Tekapo, and they streamed out gaily from the ridge pole of a tent …'

One of the requirements of holding such a large tract of land in the 1800s was to run a certain amount of stock on the property so, after several days, everyone, except John and Mary, returned to Pigeon Bay to bring down the stock – 40 or 50 horned cattle. This first established run in the Mackenzie was known as The Mary Range. It is now part of The Wolds.

When the others left, John and Mary were 'left alone for a time, monarchs of all we surveyed, including Mount Cook, Ben Ohau, the Liebig Ranges, and a host of smaller fry too insignificant to count in such company. Our isolation was complete. Situated in the midst of wildness and desolation, our surroundings were grand in the extreme, but somewhat overpowering in their silent lonesomeness …'

John had accompanied the first white women who ventured up the Whanganui River and the first who crossed the Christchurch Plains and settled in Canterbury. Now his wife had become the first white woman to cross the Tekapo River, and to enter and take up residence in the Mackenzie.

The couple built their wattle and daub home on the south-east side of Lake Pukaki, close to the shore. Daub is a substance commonly made from a mixture of clay mixed with straw and applied to a lattice of vertical studs and horizontal wattles to create a wall. It is on old technique, commonly used in Europe. Improvisation proved vital. 'None of the Pukaki stores happened to have any plate glass on hand just then, so for windows we used the next best thing – calico! And in lieu of the slate roof, which ought properly to have covered us with a crown of glory, we thatched ourselves in with snow-grass and drew the tarpaulin snugly over the lot.'

For the first six months, most of John's efforts were concerned with the building of their home, a shed and some yards. This involved cutting, sawing and conveying all of the timber required on his canoe, from the island to the shore, which was 'something over a mile'. The timber was too heavy to raft across, and their canoe was only able to manage three posts or a few sticks of timber, and several spars fastened to the outer part of the canoe, on each trip. He often got into strife when the wind blew up and the canoe filled with water, but always managed to complete his journey.

But a 'curious and startling' adventure with a young visiting relative named Jim nearly proved fatal. On their way back from the island a brisk wind blew up, the water became choppy and the canoe began to fill with water. They could neither go back against the wind nor continue forward – and Jim could not swim. They needed to jettison their cargo, and managed to remove some of it, but the canoe then settled into the water stern first, with its bow, to which Jim was clinging, in the air. Using the woollen jersey he was wearing, John secured his visitor to the boat and then, straddling him and the bow, eventually, through some herculean effort, managed to paddle the 'perpendicular canoe' to shore. They were so 'dead beat' that they lay on the beach, wet clothes and all, and 'slept soundly for over two hours from sheer and utter exhaustion'.

An early photo of a car at the end of Lake Pukaki, before the lake was raised, and close to Mary and John McHutcheson's home. HAVELOCK WILLIAMS

Some time later, John and another young relative called William but known as 'Canterbury Bill', or 'CB' for short, canoed down the rapids of a flooded creek, capsized, managed to right the vessel and were disgorged into Lake Pukaki. Having lost both paddles, they used CB's 'new and stiff Wellington boots' to row to the island, where they fashioned proper paddles. The distance was short but the 'spectacle of two full-grown men gravely propelling a canoe along with a pair of knobby knee boots was so irresistibly comical that we several times lay on our leather oars and laughed till the tears came'.

The only garden John and Mary attempted was on the island, to be free of weka and rats and to provide some shelter, but 'it was a poor venture, even in its prime'. Severe weather and poor soil meant that only a few of the vegetables survived. They made up for this by living quite well on weka and grey and paradise ducks. There were also small fish like perch in Lake Pukaki, although not present in any great numbers.

At one point, supplies became very low when fresh provisions, due with the rest of the group, had not arrived. 'Our bill of fare was reduced to rice and a little sugar, upon which we subsisted entirely for a fortnight or so. No tea, no flour, no meat, no mustard even to vary the monotonous dish.' John decided to journey to Timaru, 80 kilometres away, to meet the supplies. He was forced to walk, as all their horses were absent, taken to help drive the cattle down from Canterbury.

He stayed the night in Timaru, keeping an eye out for Francis and the rest of the team and, on finding no sign of them, he set out to walk back the following day with a 13-kilogram swag of supplies, including a leg of mutton, on his back. At 7 p.m. he stopped on the banks of the Tekapo River for supper with his dog, and, although he was very tired, the stunning grandeur of his surroundings did not escape him:

It was a lovely moonlight night, clear as the noonday. The scene was a striking one, and imprinted itself indelibly on my memory … At my feet swept a powerful mountain current, glittering with moonbeams flashing noisily in its ripples, its calm dark eddies showing depths of unfathomable blue as they faithfully and brilliantly mirrored the star-spangled vault above. All around us rose the grand everlasting hills whose every clear-cut peak stood out in bold relief against the cloudless sky, while over all and above all loomed up the great white throne of the snowy crests beyond. Such my kitchen and banqueting hall, such my surroundings, as I cooked and ate my humble dinner-and-tea supper that night. Surely never did king or emperor banquet himself with grander surroundings …

After supper he attempted to cross the river, intending to camp on the other side for the night, but was swept off his feet by the current and, swag and all, carried downstream. 'Too wet and miserable to go to sleep', he pushed on and finally, after covering another 30 kilometres, staggered home by midnight. 'I should like to be able to say that I rose next morning with the lark none the worse for my exploit, but the truth is I was so thoroughly done up that I lay in bed for 30 hours afterwards too wearied to move a limb or wink an eye.'

Being so far from civilisation meant serious risks if things went wrong. A sprained ankle today is not dangerous, but in the 1850s, without a horse, and with a wife or husband anywhere within a 100-kilometre radius, the situation could become life threatening. At one stage, while exploring up towards Lake Ohau and the Benmore ranges, John was thrown from his horse. He landed on rocks and was knocked semi-conscious. He lay there for some time bleeding heavily from a large gash on his head. Luckily, he regained enough consciousness to stumble back to a hut, around 25 kilometres away. In later years, pioneers would light fires to signal trouble and attract help, but that was difficult for the first settlers, as there was no one there to see them.

To be the first to arrive in an area like the Mackenzie was fraught with challenges, but it was also full of exciting discoveries. John was amazed by the amount of moa bones he discovered, many of them 'right on the surface of the ground' and several heaps that seemed to be only a few years old. In fact he felt they were so recent that, when exploring a new region or secluded valley, he found himself keeping a 'weather eye open' for a live specimen. But in those early days they had 'neither the time nor the inclination for the study of extinct animals; it was all we could do to

Lake Pukaki and the Ben Ohau Range, early winter. MARY HOBBS

preserve our own species from being wiped out'. Although John had no luck in finding moa, he did discover, in a secluded valley between Tekapo and Pukaki, a very woolly sheep, left behind by Mackenzie, the infamous sheep stealer, after whom the area is named. He reported the fleece to be 17 or 18 inches – 43 to 46 centimetres – in length.

Mary McHutcheson remained in the area for almost a year but returned to Pigeon Bay when she became pregnant. Her husband remained on the run to try and make a go of it but was alone for most of that time. John described their life at Pukaki as very hard, and some of their experiences 'the reverse of pleasant', but remarked that 'on the whole we enjoyed ourselves as most people do who work hard and sleep sound'. He persevered for two years, but his nephew Francis was ready to quit the property and provisionally found Magistrate John Watson and Henry Gladstone of Akaroa willing purchasers. Gladstone had accompanied them on their first trip to The Mary Range and returned to Christchurch, where he then applied for the run west of Pukaki, which later became known as Rhoborough Downs. The Mary Range was then purchased by William Saunders and combined with The Wolds

John later acknowledged that he wasn't deeply in love with the Mackenzie, but he was determined to give it a fair trial and would certainly have done so had his nephew, Francis, not been so keen to quit the station. When he 'counted up the cost', he found that the only 'set-off against a considerable loss of capital was a treasury of experiences, and a memory of adventure much easier to talk about than to go through'. However, when he gazed at the painting in the Dunedin exhibition, old memories came 'crowding back with a rush':

> Pukaki! Bless me, so it is, and a capital picture, too; and there is giant Aorangi, the sublime cloud piercer! How grandly that noble shoulder of naked granite used to bulk up against the great white throne behind! How gloriously those domes of frosted silver were wont to catch up the first rosy beams of returning day! How those majestic peaks shone in all their splendour as the rising sun chased the golden tints of orange and pink across their spotless summits!

As the first white woman to enter and settle in the Mackenzie Country,

Mary McHutcheson is well remembered geographically through the Mary Range and Maryburn Stream, which travellers on State Highway 8 cross over today. There is a Mount Mary in the vicinity, now with a repeater aerial on its summit. Simon, one of the Maori who travelled with the first party, is remembered in Simons Hill and Simons Pass stations.

In 1858, once the station was sold, John made his way to Nelson, where his son was born, and bought into a gold claim at the Collingwood diggings. After injuring both legs and his ribs, and failing to make his fortune, John returned to farming, this time in the Wairau. In 1859 the couple moved to Blenheim, where John, by now known as John Mack Hutcheson (an alternative name he had used on his wedding certificate),[5] became the fourth mayor in 1874. He lived to a good age, dying in January 1899, at the age of 82.

During his long and varied life John came to understand the value of friendship:

> True friends are among the most precious things of this earth, hard to get, difficult to keep, but when secured worth all the trouble of keeping. Precious are they in youth, doubly precious in life's prime, but precious most of all when the sere and yellow leaf begins to fall. Incessant change is perhaps the most striking characteristic of colonial life, yet here and there even in New Zealand a contented spirit may be found who has taken root so kindly and firmly that the restless sea of colonial life beats round them in vain; landmarks they are in an ocean of unrest.

Today, there is no sign of where the McHutchesons built their wattle and daub home on the south-east shore of Lake Pukaki. Yet, in the twenty-first century, people remain enchanted by the stunning beauty of the crystal-clear waters, with Aoraki/Mt Cook in the distance, just as John and Mary were, over 150 years ago.

OPPOSITE An island in Lake Pukaki, before the lake was raised. FREDERICK GEORGE RADCLIFFE, ALEXANDER TURNBULL LIBRARY, WELLINGTON, NEW ZEALAND
OVERLEAF The Ben Ohau Range, close to the first home built in the Mackenzie Country. MARY HOBBS

Lake Pukaki, Showing Mt Cook 40 miles away. N.Z.F.G.R. 5551.

BIRCH HILL

Nicolo 'Big Mick' Radove, of Birch Hill Station, slowly made his way up to the top of a small hill behind his modest cob cottage, carefully carrying his best mate, John 'Jimmy' Lloyd, in his arms.[1] Jimmy was terminally ill, but each evening he liked to see the sun set over Mount Cook, so Mick would wrap him in a blanket and take him to his favourite spot. Together they watched as the sun cast a dazzling array of bright golden pinks across the vast canvas of snow-capped mountains, before slowly fading into softer shades of violet and indigo, and then slipping behind the peaks of the Main Divide. Mick would then return Jimmy to the warmth of the house and stoke up the fire as the cold, dark night closed in.

The two men first met on the shearing circuit in the high country and formed a strong friendship, usually working together. Mick was a record-setter, able to shear 50 merinos before, depending on which account you read, breakfast or lunch.[2] His real name was Nicolo Radove; he had gained the nickname of 'Big Mick' while working at sea. Said to have been born in Palermo, Sicily around 1834, he served in the Royal Navy, starting out as a cabin boy, and fought in the Crimean War, where he survived the bitterly cold winter months of the cruel siege of Sebastopol. He was wounded and nursed back to health in one of the camps established by Florence Nightingale.[3] He later named a 1200-metre peak on

Mount Sefton and The Footstool in late summer from what was formerly Birch Hill Station. MARY HOBBS

Birch Hill Station, Mount Sebastopol. It is just above Black Birch Stream, approximately 7 kilometres from the first Birch Hill homestead, and has a spectacular view from the summit.

After gold mining in Australia, Mick made his way to New Zealand in 1858 (or possibly 1860) and worked for several years as a station hand at Ben Ohau, Benmore and Lake Ohau stations.

ABOVE 'Big Mick's Homestead, Birch Hill', circa 1869. SOUTH CANTERBUY MUSEUM
OPPOSITE The inscription on John (Jimmy) Lloyd's grave. MARY HOBBS

George Hodgkinson, already running Lake Ohau, applied for the Birch Hill run in 1865 and arranged for his station hands to manage the property on his behalf. One of those men was Mick, who eventually scraped together enough money to purchase it in 1871. Although not the first owner, he was the first to live there and call it home. He became a well-known figure in the Mackenzie and was a favourite in the district, known for his 'unfailing good temper and kindness of heart'.[4]

Birch Hill originally extended up to the glaciers and included the area where the first Hermitage was later built, as well as the eventual site of

Aoraki/Mount Cook Village. Mick regularly clambered up mountains in the vicinity, not in the pursuit of sport, but in pursuit of his sheep. There is an old story of Dr Julius Haast climbing the southern spur of Mount Cook and remarking to his surveyor companion that no one had been higher on this mountain than them. Almost before he had finished the sentence, a shout was heard from above. Haast could have been forgiven for thinking it was a visitation from on high, but it was just Big Mick, warning them not to disturb his sheep.[5]

When Mick moved to Birch Hill, it was inevitable that his mate Jimmy Lloyd would turn up to give him a hand. Together they mustered in this wild, spectacular territory, sharing the good times and the bad, while putting their hearts into earning a living. After several challenging years on the station, Jimmy gradually tired more easily, until a doctor's appointment in Timaru confirmed that he had little time left to live, so he returned to Birch Hill and spent his last days with Mick, who nursed him until the end. He was just 36 when he died on 16 September 1872.

In his *Jubilee History of South Canterbury*, Johannes Andersen reports that a distraught Mick laid his healthy body on top of Jimmy's and desperately tried to breathe life back into him.[6] As his mate had requested, Mick buried him at the spot where they had sat together each night. He also erected a wooden picket fence around the perimeter of the grave. Over the more than 140 years since Jimmy's death, sheep have probably been the most frequent visitors to this peaceful spot. The headstone, faded now, still stands proudly at the head of the grave, testimony to a great friendship. The Department of Conservation respectfully cares for this historic site, placing hay around the headstone during the harsh winter months to help protect it from the elements.

The Burnetts of Mount Cook Station, Mick's closest neighbours on the east side of the Tasman River, thought highly of the big man and had helped to advise him on the station's management. A protruding rock on their station is named Mick's Point. It lies directly opposite Birch Hill and is so named because when Andrew Burnett had a message for Mick, he lit a fire there to attract his attention, so he could ride over.

In late January 1873 Governor Sir George Bowen arrived in the South Island with an adventurous itinerary that included Mount Cook, the glaciers and several local high country stations. His trip was well described

by a special correspondent for the *Timaru Herald*, who travelled with the VIP party and wrote a full and lively account of the journey, which was intrepid, even if the governor did have his own personal servant. After visiting other stations, and admiring the spectacular scenery, the party of seven arrived near Mount Cook, made camp and immediately set off to explore the Mueller and Tasman glaciers. Then they were joined by Big Mick, who had taken supplies to their camp and then rode up to the Tasman Glacier to meet the governor.[7] It was a great joy for Mick when Bowen spoke to him in Italian. Sir George's wife was Italian and the Bowens conversed in Italian at home, so the governor was fluent. Both men enjoyed this novel experience in such a remote location.

On the way back to camp, Mick took the visitors to see the Blue and Green Lakes, described by the *Herald* reporter as 'pretty lagoons which lie between the present glacier and an ancient moraine on the western side of the valley, and by the peaceful aspect of their still, blue waters, afford a striking contrast to the rugged surroundings'.[8] These small lakes still delight locals seeking a refreshing swim in summer, though there are tales of small, hairy native fish that are known to give bathers a gentle nip.

ABOVE The first Hermitage, which was built on Birch Hill Station. JACK ADAMSON COLLECTION

OPPOSITE En route to the summit of Mount Sebastopol. MARY HOBBS

The following day Governor Bowen and his party departed and Mick 'kindly came to see us safely over the [Tasman] river, which we crossed at a very good ford'.[10] As he said goodbye, Sir George made a special request to Mick to save the bush near where they had camped, so that future generations could also enjoy it. Mick wholeheartedly agreed. It was labelled a special reserve and, to this day, visitors to Aoraki/Mount Cook National Park can walk through this virgin forest at Bowen Bush and Governor's Bush and enjoy it just as His Excellency did in 1873.

Mick had little patience with some of the other early travellers who arrived at Birch Hill on their way to see the glaciers and Mount Cook, as apparently some took it almost for granted that they could call in, eat any dinner Mick may have cooking and then set up camp and kill sheep from his flock to sustain themselves during their stay. Some days, he was heard to say that he wished they would take Mount Cook with them on their backs so he would not have to be troubled by them any more.[11]

Although Mick mainly worked alone, cadets would arrive to help out, as for several years Birch Hill had been known as an ideal training ground for those keen to become more experienced in high country farming. In 1874, 28-year-old William S. Wilkin had just completed his time at Birch Hill and rode up to the homestead, where he tethered his horse. He gave his horse a tap on the rump as he passed it on his way to the cottage, at which point the startled animal lashed out with its hoof, kicking the young man in the stomach. Big Mick immediately came out and carried William, who was conscious, inside. Nothing seemed immediately wrong, but over a day or so his condition markedly deteriorated. A station hand was sent to fetch Dr Frederick Kimbell, who owned Three Springs Station, but arrived to find that he was in Timaru. William Wilkin died the next day, 5 March, and Mick had the sad task of burying him close to Jimmy's grave. Several months later, William's family arranged for William's body to be exhumed and he was reburied at Burkes Pass Cemetery, where the epitaph on his gravestone includes a poignant message of appreciation to those who helped to bring him to his final resting place. The dip in the ground where William was originally interred remains as an unspoken reminder of the tragedy. Perhaps this was too much for Mick, as later that year he sold Birch Hill for a good price and left the area.

A series of different owners bought and sold Birch Hill Station until

With his friendly nature, Mick made the perfect guide. As they meandered back to camp, he pointed out the southern spur of Mount Cook, which he had once crossed in search of his sheep. Old stories mention that on one occasion Mick was out for three nights in a storm with no food, except for the roots of snowgrass that he found to sustain him. He eventually made his way over from the Tasman Glacier to the Hooker and, according to one source, was the first man to cross the Mount Cook Range.[9]

1883, when Duncan Sutherland of Omarama Station became the sole owner. The manager, Alexander McKinnon, had married Kate Munro, the eldest daughter of W.G. Munro of Otematata Hotel in the Waitaki Valley, on 25 August 1881. They had a daughter, Margaret, born in 1883 and Kate was expecting their second child. But in December that year Alexander was hit by a falling rock while out mustering. His station hands managed to get him to Timaru, but he died from his injuries on 11 January 1884, aged only 28. He was buried in the tiny Otematata cemetery. Alexander, named after his father, was born later that year.

George Sutherland, a relation of Duncan, then managed Birch Hill for several years. He was favourably mentioned in *The High Alps of New Zealand* by the Reverend William Spotswood Green, who, with Emil Boss and Ulrich Kaufmann, was intent on being the first to summit Mount Cook in 1882. Caught in a storm on their way to the mountain, the trio took refuge at Birch Hill for a night. A couple also arrived at Birch Hill to see the glaciers, so George found himself with five unexpected guests on the same evening. He cheerfully brewed tea, fed and found shelter for them all. The next day he killed a sheep for the Green party and even rode up to their camp to deliver it. He also gave them a hand on their return after their failed attempt to climb Mount Cook.

The winter of 1895 was the most severe on record and Birch Hill did not escape its fury. Almost all the stock was wiped out, a devastating blow. The property was offered for lease, with the Hermitage accommodation, for £110, but there were no takers, so it was abandoned in 1896.

Between the years of 1897 and 1912 there were a series of different owners, until the station was eventually purchased by Henry Le Cren. From this point on, Birch Hill was run in conjunction with Glentanner Station, as E.R. Guinness (Glentanner) and Le Cren (Birch Hill) were also partners in an auctioneering business, although they owned their stations separately. Birch Hill Station is now part of Aoraki/Mount Cook National Park.

And Big Mick? He travelled to the North Island in search of new land, but found nothing to his liking. With encouragement from his old

neighbour, Andrew Burnett, he returned to the Mackenzie in 1875 and purchased the Mistake Station, now known as Godley Peaks, remotely situated on the north-west side of Lake Tekapo, at the head of the lake. Mick had done well with the sale of Birch Hill and was generous with his good fortune. The parties he held at the Mistake Station were said to have lasted for a week or longer. If the beer ran out, Mick would ride down to Tekapo and return with more.

The highest point of the Mistake Station is Mount Radove, at 2430 metres. Most of the station is over 900 metres above sea level, so Mick had made a substantial investment in one of the harshest environments of the South Island, and the following ten years were to be some of his toughest. By 1878 the money had dwindled and in 1879 a substantial snowfall caused a great many stock losses.

But in that year, too, Mick married Ellen Fleming, originally from Ireland. More order was restored to the station after his marriage. The couple had a daughter, Annie Maria, in October 1880, but she died two months later, on 10 December. Their second daughter, Catherine, died on 1 December 1881, at the age of just four months. The infants are buried beside each other in the picturesque Burkes Pass Cemetery.

At some time after this, a niece of Ellen's from Ireland, Nora Quinn, born in 1870, was left an orphan after her mother died. The family had emigrated to New Zealand from County Kerry and settled in Timaru in 1874. Ellen and Mick took Nora in. In 1893 she married Jack Adamson, the country's first New Zealand-born mountain guide. They lived at the Hermitage, where Nora managed the accommodation and meals. She had become an exceptional horsewoman while living at the Mistake Station and was regarded as the best in the area. After her first son was born in Fairlie in 1894, Nora was returning home on horseback, with the reins in one hand and her baby in the other, when she arrived at The Twins Stream and was dismayed to find it in flood. Local drovers implored her to return to Fairlie but Nora spurred her horse on and successfully crossed the river, leaving the men, mouths agape, in her wake, as she set off to return safely to the Hermitage.[12]

The Long Depression of the 1880s meant falling prices and another substantial snowstorm in 1884 caused more stock losses. From the time he purchased the Mistake Station, Mick had struggled and his debts

35

continued to escalate. The owners of Mick's mortgage, the National Mortgage and Agency Company, sold the station. They gave Mick no warning and there was no consultation. As a result, the Radoves were forced to leave their home in 1885, but not without a fight. Incensed by the callous treatment, Mick fought the injustice in court and won, as the mortgage company had given insufficient notice. Unfortunately the mortgagees made a counter-claim and Big Mick's win was reduced to a pittance.

In *Early South Canterbury Runs*, Robert Pinney wrote of 'the tragedy of a magnificent, virile, but unlettered man, facing mortgages, liens, bills and powers of sale, and all that entanglement against which it is so hope-less to fight'.[13] After a short stay in Timaru, Ellen and Mick moved to the Hermitage, where Nora and Jack found jobs for them. As a guide, Mick 'was a great favourite with tourist visitors as he had been in the old days with his neighbours'. He was later described as 'a rough diamond, indeed, but kind of heart, and when in a position to play the host, hospitable to a notable degree, even in a region where hospitality is a sacred duty'.[14]

Within eight years of the Radoves losing their two infant daugh-ters and the Mistake Station, Big Mick returned to Timaru in ill health. Initially he suffered from a liver complaint, but later died from the rup-ture of a blood vessel in his intestine[15] on 30 July 1888, aged 54. Although, Robert Pinney suggests that he died from a broken heart. Nicolo Radove's death was widely reported in the South Island and the legend of Big Mick, with his great physical presence and his equally great heart, lives on.

LEFT Jack and Nora Adamson outside the Hermitage, with their first-born son, John. JACK ADAMSON COLLECTION

OPPOSITE Early visitors to the Mueller Glacier. JACK ADAMSON COLLECTION

MOUNT COOK
STATION

In 1864, a bullock wagon carrying four people emerged at the top of a large hill in the Mackenzie high country, briefly silhouetted against the fading light. Andrew and Catherine Burnett and their two children, Catherine Mackay, known as Miss Kitty, age two, and Donald, just 12 months, braced themselves as, with the wheels locked, Andrew carefully guided the wagon down a sharp zigzag to the valley floor below.

They had made their way through the Maryburn Valley to avoid the perils of the Tasman River, known to have quicksand in places. There was no track to follow. They had endured a rough, bumpy ride over undulating terrain peppered with prickly matagouri, sharp spaniards, tussock and boulders. They crossed the Jollie River and finally drew up at the homestead at dusk, weary from the long journey. In *High Endeavour,* William Vance describes the Burnetts' first home as a 'one-room hut of black birch logs plastered with clay and thatched with snowgrass'.[1]

Mount Cook Station is situated at the head of the Tasman Valley, between the Jollie and Tasman rivers, on the east side of Lake Pukaki, opposite Glentanner and Birch Hill. The Tasman River is the property's western boundary; its northern boundary was originally near the Tasman Glacier. New Zealand's highest peaks lie beyond.

Even for a strong person like Catherine Burnett, the landscape was daunting. The following day, as she surveyed her surroundings in more

Looking towards the Burnett Range and Mount Cook Station from the west.
MARY HOBBS

has always been a haven for native birds as they drink the nectar from its fragrant spring flowers and nestle in its thickets. Native plants also find shelter and protection beneath its prickly branches.

Andrew Burnett and Catherine Mackay were married on 26 May 1861 at Achrimsdale, in Clyne Parish, Sutherland, Scotland. Andrew, born in 1838, listed his occupation as a shepherd. Catherine, who was about a year older, was a dairymaid. Fewer than six weeks later, on 3 July, the young couple set off for the other side of the world, leaving behind all they knew and loved in Scotland. On 8 October, they arrived at Lyttelton on the *Royal Stuart*. They were to remain in New Zealand for the rest of their lives.

Andrew's skills as a shepherd were in great demand. Over the next few years he managed Grays Hills Station and then Blue Cliffs. Later, while managing Simons Pass Station, on the south-eastern side of Lake Pukaki, he discovered that the land that later became Mount Cook Station had not yet been claimed. He and George McRae quickly lodged a submission for the original lease of the 6000-hectare property known as Run 498.[4] Andrew bought his partner out several years later. William Vance says that McRae, who applied in Christchurch on behalf of both men, came up with the station's name on the spur of the moment.

A condition of the pastoral leases was that they had to be stocked, but getting the sheep or cattle to a run without roads was a challenge. While the land was being stocked, the building of sheds and a more substantial homestead was also a priority. Most of the original houses were made of thatched cob.

Initially there was just a camp oven to cook on, and living conditions were primitive and tough, especially for women. Catherine's day would have begun at daybreak with baking fresh bread, feeding the family and the station hands, milking the cow and, on several days of the week, churning butter and making cream. The vegetable garden had to be looked after, as well as the hens. Most clothing was made at home, socks were darned and other clothing mended, washed, ironed (with flat irons heated on the coal range) and sometimes starched.

High country women often gave birth alone, or with the assistance of their husband or, if he were away, anyone in the vicinity, usually a man. Catherine and Andrew had eight children. Miss Kitty, born in 1862, and

detail, she marvelled at how they ever managed to make their way down that 'fearsome hill' in one piece and how they would ever get back out again.[2]

The landscape was harsh, yet also breathtakingly beautiful. Early explorers Charles Torlesse and Julius Haast both mentioned the vigorous growth of Wild Irishman (or matagouri, *Discaria toumatou*) and spaniard (or speargrass, *Aciphylla colensoi*), which were capable of stabbing a person from every angle and made travelling on horseback almost impossible. Haast reported seeing matagouri as high as 5.5 metres and over 60 centimetres wide. After an initial burn, good grass began to grow, but the matagouri stood firm for a long time afterwards. As the Burnetts later wryly commented, 'In its early years more wool was shorn from the sheep on the Run by the Irishmen than by the Scotsmen.'[3] Yet the matagouri

ABOVE Pencil drawings of Andrew and Catherine Burnett, drawn by one of their daughters, circa 1899. SOUTH CANTERBURY MUSEUM
OPPOSITE Mount Cook homestead. Andrew Burnett pulls the wagon, while Kitty holds T.D. Burnett. Donald Burnett (senior) standing. Also present are Johanna and Andrew Burnett junior, among others. MRS P.R. WOODHOUSE

Donald, who followed a year later, Mary Jane in 1866, Betsy, born in Otaio, South Canterbury in 1867, and Johanna, born in 1871. Another son, Andrew, was also born that year. Jessie Agnes was born in 1874 and a third son, Thomas David, in 1877. To ensure that their children had easier access to schools during the winter, when the family was not at the station, Catherine and Andrew purchased a property at Cave in 1872 and a house in Perth Street, Timaru, four years later.

Most of Andrew's shepherds stayed for many years. One of his most valued managers, who remained with the Burnetts for decades, was Bill Seymour, who later purchased Ferintosh Station.

In the later part of the nineteenth century increasing numbers of tourists travelled to the area to view the scenic grandeur of the glaciers.

Most visitors anticipated food and shelter at Mount Cook Station and provisions for the day of their departure. When, in early February 1873, Governor Bowen and his entourage arrived at the station en route to the glaciers, he was, wrote the 'special reporter' for the *Timaru Herald*, 'hospitably received' by the Burnetts, with Andrew showing them the best place to ford the Tasman River. (There were about 22 different streams lying between Mount Cook Station and Birch Hill on the other side, so it was good to know the right crossing points.) The house, it was noted, sat 'at the foot of a hill, on which the grass was so verdant as to remind one forcibly of the rich English downs, and the fatness of the mutton bore testimony to the excellence of the grass as sheep feed'.[5] Another group arrived at the station that year, also on their way to visit the glaciers.

Among them was Joanna Harper, wife of barrister, explorer and later MP Leonard Harper, the first white woman, other than their mother, that the Burnett children had seen. She fondly recalled Catherine catering for their large party and how she enjoyed the novelty of talking with another woman.[6]

More visitors found their way to the station in 1878. One trio arrived in the midst of a storm but declined kind invitations to stay, as they wanted to get over the Tasman River before it became too high. Andrew insisted they take bread and mutton with them, as he doubted they would be able to light a fire once they reached the other side. He was right, and once they had made camp the men were very grateful for his generosity and foresight.

In 1882, on their way to attempt to summit Mount Cook, William Spotswood Green, Emil Boss and Ulrich Kaufmann stayed at the station. In his book, *The High Alps of New Zealand*, Green recalled Catherine's kindness in supplying them with a substantial meal while Andrew instructed one of his shepherds to help them ford the Tasman River and avoid the dangerous quicksands. By this time Catherine and Andrew were living in their second home built on the station, a two-room cob house. Green described it as a 'long, low, thatched cottage, in which the family reside during the summer when sheep-shearing is the great work of life, returning to their permanent home in Timaru before the winter snows set in, and thus spending their summer in as health-giving and enjoyable a manner as it is possible to imagine.' He also wrote of the garden beside the house, 'thickly planted with gooseberry trees and squares of useful vegetables'.[7] Years later a third, much more substantial, homestead was built close to the site and remains in use today.

Catherine Burnett was, in Green's words, 'full to overflowing with the happiness of her life while discussing all sorts of plans for our comfort, and descanting on the hygienic properties of the air and the sunshine'. Before the mountaineers left, she presented them with a roll of butter wrapped in a cabbage leaf, explaining that it was too hard to do without such luxuries on the long weary expedition that lay ahead. She also made sure their pockets were crammed full of hot scones, still warm from the oven, and then bid them Godspeed.

After failing to reach the summit on 2 March, by only 10 metres, Green, Boss and Kaufmann received a letter from Catherine Burnett, via George Sutherland, who was then in charge of Birch Hill Station. She said that the Burnetts would have left for the lowlands on their return, but invited them to use their house as they wished. After accepting hospitality at Birch Hill, the climbers arrived at Mount Cook Station to find 'the door ajar and cream, bread and a quarter of mutton on the table'.

Another visitor arrived, so he joined them in their feast. After dinner, the guests enjoyed gooseberries and red currants from the laden bushes in the garden before returning to the house for tea. Two more Englishmen arrived, so now there was a party of seven, including the bullock driver and George Sutherland, who had guided them safely across the Tasman River. The next day Green reported that 'Sutherland rode off on his way to his lonely home at Birch Hill, and taking our seats in the wagon we rattled over the shingle, and through the streams of the Jollie River and then over wide flats, towards Braemar sheep station.'

In addition to her hospitality with visitors, Catherine Burnett assisted others in the district who were in desperate need. She helped William Saunders of The Wolds with the care of his infant son,[8] John, after the death of his wife, Sarah, in 1876, though the little boy died of bronchitis in December of the same year. Just eight years later, the Burnetts came to know the immeasurable pain of losing a child when their son Andrew contracted scarlet fever, which developed into rheumatic fever and heart disease. He died on 2 October 1884, aged only 13.

Thomas David Burnett, known as T.D., the youngest son of Andrew and Catherine, was 17 when a devastating snowstorm caused such carnage to the high country that some runholders were bankrupted. He worked with the station hands in a desperate attempt to save the sheep. They made an impromptu snow camp, with walls that reached almost 2 metres, and set about rescuing any stock they could find. T.D. recalled layers of dead sheep stacked up, while others, barely alive, were collected into a main area. The sheep were so desperate for feed that some ate the wool from the backs of dead animals, or chewed their ears. Faced with this devastation, T.D. vowed that when he was older he would do all he could to avert such tragedy from ever occurring again. He began by fencing off the better blocks of land with sunny aspects and kept the flocks concentrated in one area in winter to reduce losses. Building on all that he knew and loved of the high country, he felt compelled to do more for the 'tussock country' man. These feelings prompted him, at the age of 42, to become an MP, representing the Temuka electorate.

In the early 1900s, Donald Burnett, T.D.'s older brother, received an inheritance from his parents, in lieu of taking over the property, and purchased Sawdon Station. This was about the same time as Catherine and Andrew Burnett retired to their Aorangi property at Cave, after having been at Mount Cook Station for about 40 years. By the time T.D. took

ABOVE T.D. Burnett when he was the MP for Temuka.
OPPOSITE Embroidery sampler created by Johanna Burnett, July 1877. SOUTH CANTERBURY MUSEUM

over Mount Cook, it covered more than 10,000 hectares, as Andrew had expanded it to include additional runs. T.D. remained at Mount Cook Station, which he ran in conjunction with other family properties including Aorangi, and Cox's Downs – next door to Mount Cook Station – and, for a time, Balmoral Station. Merinos were ideally suited to this part of the high country and T.D.'s main focus was on making his merino flock the most pure in Canterbury. T.D.'s sisters were also involved in farming, and took over the freehold of Cox's Downs in 1911. Jessie Agnes helped to manage Mount Cook Station when her brother entered politics.

T.D. was a man on a mission. In his own words, he preferred to make a decision about things now and have a row about it later if necessary.[9] He combined work on the station with public works. A strong conservationist, he constantly urged people to plant trees and to look after any they already had. He was intent on stemming erosion and creating shelter, as the harsh winds resulted in substantial soil loss and shelterbelts helped with soil preservation and protection of stock.

As an additional way of providing needed employment during the Depression of the 1930s, T.D. financed several stone memorials in the district. Not one to miss an opportunity, on some of them he left a message for future generations. One such monument was in memory of Michael John Burke, a Canterbury runholder who, in 1855, was the first European to find the route into the Mackenzie Country through the pass that bears his name. Included on the memorial are the words, 'Oh ye who enter the portals of the Mackenzie to found homes, take the word of a Child of the Misty Gorges and plant forest trees for your lives. So shall your mountain facings and river flats be preserved [for] your children's children and for evermore. 1917.' By the year of T.D.'s death in 1941, there were approximately 300,000 trees on Mount Cook Station.

T.D. was not so friendly towards kea. In his day, the mountain parrots were present in such numbers that they became a constant danger to the sheep, pecking their backs to eat their fat and killing them. The *Jubilee History of South Canterbury*, published in 1916, reported that kea killed an average of 500 sheep on Mount Cook Station every year.[10] War was declared on the birds, and the government then offered 5 shillings for each kea head. (Different bounties were set over the years.) This hunting drove the kea back into higher alpine regions.

When Julius Haast, as provincial geologist, was exploring in this area in 1862, he commented on the substantial number of kea, which flew in flocks of four to eight. Apparently, in the early days, kea were strictly vegetarian, but with the arrival of sheep their natural habits quickly changed. Haast noted that the kea were often accompanied by kaka, as well as another similar bird with a more brilliant colour. He also observed numbers of mountain ducks, including paradise ducks, and weka, and, as the *Jubilee History* noted, he had the good fortune to see, on only a few occasions, a bird of prey 'as large as a good-sized eagle'.[11] Haast and his companions were woken by the numerous birds of the dawn chorus, which included what were then known as New Zealand thrushes, or piopio, and bellbirds.

When the Duke of Bedford presented thar to the New Zealand government in 1904, T.D. was aware they would be destructive to the environment and hunted them down to halt the problem before it became larger. He killed one at a spot on Mount Cook Station that later became known as Thar Rock. Afterwards it is said he vowed that if he had the time he would have shot the lot.[12]

Rabbits created substantial damage to the high country while T.D. was based at Mount Cook Station and he used his influence to help eradicate them by becoming the first chairman of the effective Tekapo Rabbit Board. He was also at the forefront of many community projects, including the establishment of the Tekapo Sales, which became an annual event not to be missed. Less commonly known is the Strathcona Hostel he established for training young women in the art of homecraft so that they could be employed to assist on farms and stations in the district. T.D. supplied both a large area of land for the hostel and the finance to run it.

Between 1938 and 1940, T.D. instigated the Downlands Water Supply Scheme, which created a good supply of water to the previously drought-prone hill country west of Timaru, with many people having reason to be grateful for it. T.D. also realised how straightforward it would be to create hydro-electric power through the lakes in the district.

Gorilla Stream Hut on Mount Cook Station, probably taken in the 1930s. FRANK MILNE COLLECTION

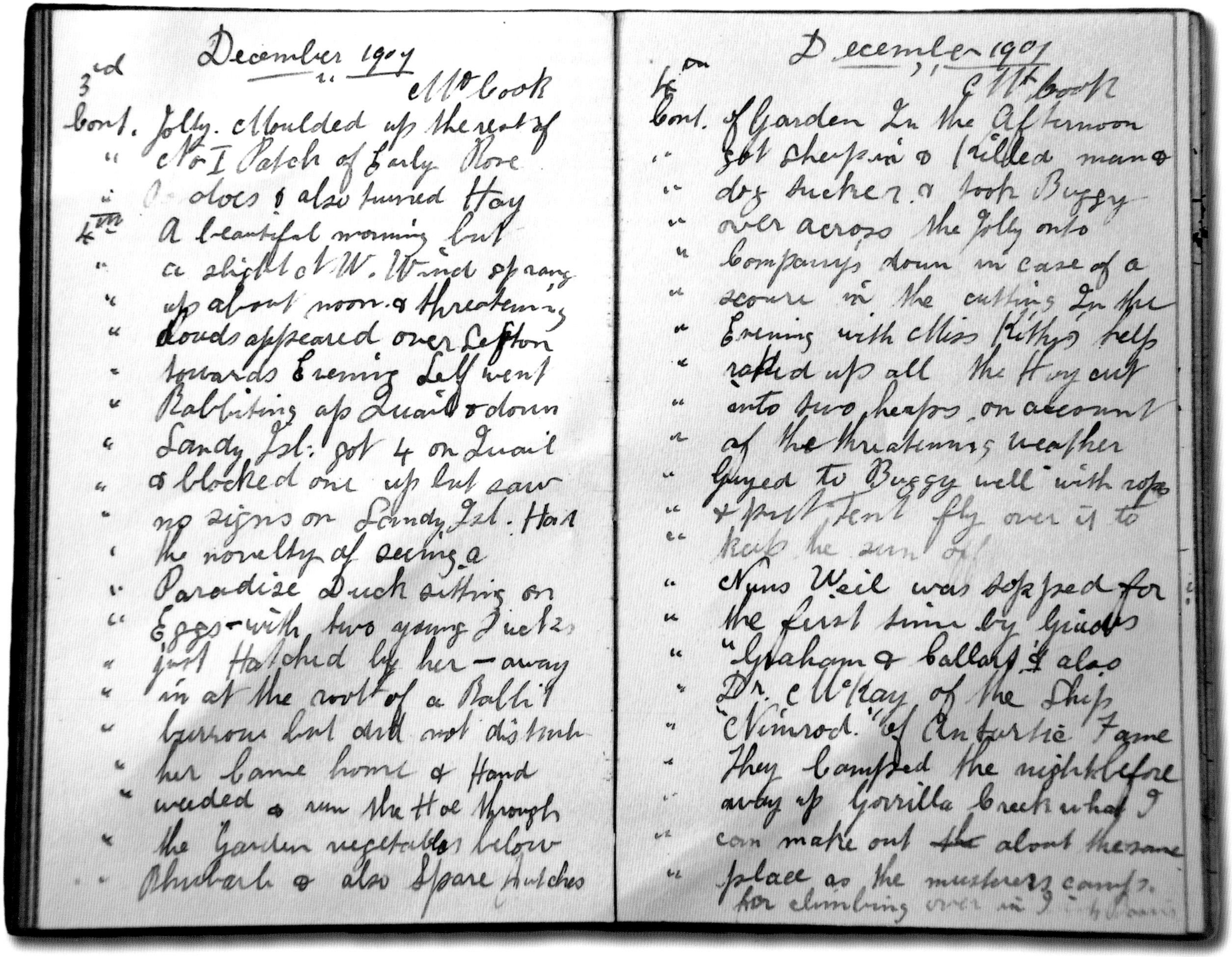

December 1907

3rd
cont. jolly. Moulded up the rest of
" No I Patch of Early Rose
" Potatoes & also turned Hay
4th A beautiful morning but
" a slight S.W. Wind sprang
" up about noon & threatening
" clouds appeared over Sefton
" towards Evening Self went
" Rabbiting up Quail & down
" Sandy Isl: got 4 on Quail
" & blocked one up but saw
" no signs on Sandy Isl. Had
" the novelty of seeing a
" Paradise Duck sitting on
" Eggs — with two young Ducks
" just Hatched by her — away
" in at the root of a Rabbit
" burrow but did not disturb
" her Came home & Hand
" weeded & ran the Hoe through
" the Garden vegetables below
" Rhubarb & also Spare Hutches

December 1907

4th
cont. of Garden In the Afternoon
" Got Shepin & killed man &
" dog Tucker & took Buggy
" over across the Jolly onto
" Companys down in case of a
" scour in the cutting In the
" Evening with Miss Kittys help
" raked up all the Hay cut
" into two heaps, on account
" of the threatening weather
" Guyed to Buggy well with rope
" & put tent fly over it to
" keep the sun off
" Nuns Weil was dossed for
" the first time by Guides
" "Graham & ballar & also
" Dr McKay of the Ship
" "Nimrod " of Antartic fame
" They Camped the night before
" away of Gorilla Creek what I
" can make out the about the same
" place as the musterers camps
" for climbing over in ...

ABOVE An extract from the journal Bill Seymour kept while working at Mount Cook Station in 1907. GILBERT SEYMOUR COLLECTION

OPPOSITE Photographer Havelock Williams poses for a photo at Kea Hut on Mount Cook Station. The photo shows the fence erected to stop the spread of rabbits. HAVELOCK WILLIAMS AND H. ANDERSON

Less popular was his decision to purchase the Tekapo Hotel, then known as Takapo House, and let the licence run out, making it a 'dry' inn, so the area's workers, without temptation, would remain sober and turn up for work on time.[13] Eventually it was sold again and the licence was restored, much to the relief of the locals. He also gave land for a road that bypassed the hotel at Cave, which bullock drivers and shearers often visited on their way to the Mackenzie. Whenever they did stop at the pub they would invariably turn up to the station a day or two behind schedule. Prohibition Road, as it is known, still exists, though it is unclear whether the men ever used it.

T.D. was a tough man. Legend has it that his son Donald was not permitted to sit too close to the fire in case it made him soft. If men on horseback came to a river on the station they could all cross on horseback, except for Donald, who was instructed to make his own way across on foot. His middle name was Mount Cook, and T.D. told his teachers at Timaru High School to address him as 'Mount Cook', so he would always remember where his priorities lay. Of course his fellow pupils shortened this to 'Cookie'.

The men who worked for T.D. were expected to measure up to his high standards. His June 1928 advertisement for 'a youth of 17 to 18 years' read: 'Must hate town life. Must weigh not less than eleven stone. Must stand cold like an Arctic Hero. Must have plenty of common sense – brains not necessary. Must be medically fit. Undersigned will be on deck 2 to 4 p.m. Saturday 13th June 1928. T.D. Burnett, Perth Street, Timaru.' Another advertisement for shepherds included the requirements: 'Mustn't have a car. Must have dogs. Stay five years.'[14]

John Scott of Godley Peaks won T.D. over when he began his job by walking from Cave Railway Station over a large hill, known as Cave Hill, to Burnett's land at Aorangi.[15] Another shepherd arrived at Fairlie, which was as far as the train went and, since there was no one to meet him, walked the 125 kilometres to Mount Cook Station with his dogs. When he finally arrived, and explained how he had travelled, T.D. said it was a good job that he had walked, as he would not have got the job otherwise.

But he did not expect others to do anything he was not willing to do himself. On several occasions, he walked from Cave to Timaru to attend a debating meeting and back again, a return journey of about 68 kilometres. He was also known to do a full day's work on the land and then ride on horseback all night to a remote part of the district so he could be there by daybreak to inspect roading. Nor would he think anything of making a 130-kilometre trip on horseback to get from the family farm at Cave to Mount Cook Station that night.[16] William Vance also reported that T.D. 'gave special attention to the welfare of his men, and it was while searching for musterers who had become benighted that his horse, stumbling against a wire fence in the darkness, fell with him. That fall, in 1924, started an illness that partially, and for long periods, wholly, incapacitated him for the next 18 years.'[17]

T.D. worked hard for the community and on the family stations. He mucked in with his men and helped to snow-rake in the big snowstorms. He also served on the local council. He had no patience for too much dependence on the government, saying, 'if too many gathered around the old milk cow she would go dry.'[18]

One of T.D.'s most impressive legacies is St David's Pioneer Memorial Church, built near the township of Cave in 1930. Appropriately, St David is the patron saint of all shepherds. T.D. was involved with choosing the building materials and the interior design, which won an architectural award for Herbert Hall in 1934. The church was built in memory of T.D.'s parents, but also stands as a tribute to all Mackenzie Country pioneers, as an inscription in the entrance porch makes clear: 'This porch is erected to the Glory of God and in memory of the sheepmen, shepherds, bullock drivers, shearers and station hands who pioneered the back country of this Province between the years 1855 and 1895.' Inside the church, a stained-glass window is dedicated to the pioneer women of the area, 'who, through Arctic winters and in the wilderness maintained their homes and kept the faith'.

The church is endearing because of the personal artefacts built into it, treasured relics from the early pioneers at Mount Cook Station and South Canterbury.[19] Local boulders are incorporated into the exterior, and, for many years, a mast lantern from an early immigrant ship hung at the entrance. A huge greywacke slab, originally used as a table in a mustering camp up the Jollie Gorge in the 1860s, is set into the wall of

---

St David's Pioneer Memorial Church, near Cave. ALLISON BENNET

the entrance. The floor is totara, the pews are rough-adzed red pine and the rafters of jarrah are wood-pegged. The walls are constructed in rough plaster, just like the walls of the old cob houses. The paving on the floor of the chancel is made of boulders from the Tasman riverbed, while the boulders that originally served as the hearth for the first Mount Cook Station homestead form part of the pulpit. An ancient totara log that was buried in the Tasman riverbed serves as the top of the pulpit. Designs of mountain lilies and ribbonwood are carved into the lectern on kowhai wood. A stone mortar used for grinding grain, which came from Scotland with the Burnetts, has a new life as part of the baptismal font, which is partly supported by an old wheel hub from the bullock wagon that carried the family to Mount Cook Station.

In 1914, after a full and active life, Catherine Burnett died at the family home in Cave. A monument in her honour, erected by T.D., stands on Mount Cook Station at the spot where she would take her prayer book and contemplate the spectacular view of the mountains. Betsy was the next member of the family to die. She had suffered from rheumatic endocarditis (inflammation of the lining of the heart) for many years and may well have caught the original fever at the same time as her brother Andrew. Despite her poor health, Betsy courageously became a nurse. She died in 1919, at the relatively young age of 52, and is buried in Timaru with her parents and her brother, Andrew. She was the only daughter not buried in the private Burnett cemetery near Cave. Andrew Burnett senior died on 21 September 1927, at the age of 89. None of the daughters married and, with the exception of Betsy, spent their lives contributing in various ways to work on the station and at home. They regularly travelled between Cave and Mount Cook Station. The oldest daughter, Catherine Mackay, died in 1938, at the age of 76.

T.D. died on 1 December 1941, aged 64. He had suffered from hydatids, which is contracted by handling dogs who have eaten raw offal from infected animals. This 'Child of the Misty Gorges', as he was called, was taken on his last journey by horse and dray and carried on the shoulders of family and trusted shepherds to his final resting place on Mount Cook Station. Bill Seymour led the way to the place known as Rock Etam, which enjoys a fine view of Aoraki/Mt Cook and the surrounding mountains.

Joanna Mackay (82), Mary Jane (87) and Donald (90) all died in 1953, and Jessie Agnes (83) in 1957. Donald and T.D. were the only children of Catherine and Andrew Burnett who married and had children. Donald married Barbara MacLeod, the schoolteacher at Burkes Pass, and they had six children. T.D. had two children, Donald and Caitriana, known as Catriona.

There is scant information about T.D.'s wife Agnes Ellen (née Little), although a lifelong friend of the family, Maureen Vance, recalls her as a strong matriarch, who was strict, yet generous too. Her family owned a large established farm near Cave. A portrait of her and her children, Donald and Catriona, commissioned by Agnes and taken at the station by renowned photographer Havelock Williams, has survived. Dressed in a simple white blouse and grey skirt, Agnes sits on the grass, poised and graceful, with Catriona on her knee, while Donald stands with a protective hand on his mother's shoulder. Agnes died 15 years after her husband, in 1956, and is buried at Pleasant Point, close to her family's farm.

Donald and Catriona Burnett spent their early years at Mount Cook Station, but when it was time for them to start school the family moved to the house in Timaru. In later years, T.D. and his wife donated the Timaru House to the city to be used as an art gallery or museum. The South Canterbury Museum now stands on the site.

After his school years, Donald returned to Mount Cook Station. Like his father, he was 26 when he took over the property. Aside from a few trips to Europe, he remained close to home and managed the station for approximately 69 years. Along with his merinos, it was his main passion.

ABOVE Donald Burnett at his home. MARY HOBBS
OPPOSITE Donald Burnett's prize merino sheep, with their coats on. MARY HOBBS

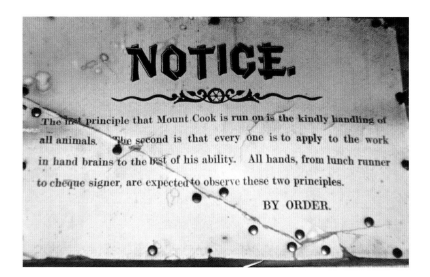

The first principle that Mount Cook is run on is the kindly handling of all animals. The second is that every one is to apply to the work in hand brains to the best of his ability. All hands, from lunch runner to cheque signer, are expected to observe these two principles.

BY ORDER.

He was of the strong belief that, when it came to sheep, the high country was the exclusive domain of merino. In fact, when local neighbour Duncan Mackenzie of Braemar brought in Perendales, Donald found it difficult to talk to him for a while. Duncan later kindly remembered Donald as a perfectionist, perhaps excessive at times, in all he did with his buildings, his fencing and the power plants he had constructed, although he thought some of Donald's newer buildings could have been better placed. He also remembered Donald hosting some field days and farm forestry days.

Donald's other interests included photography and the exploration of technology and engineering. He printed his own photos and made 16-millimetre films, recording many events, including skiing excursions in New Zealand, holidays to Europe and mustering on the station. He was such a private person that only close friends saw these photos or the film.

Donald built three powerhouses on Mount Cook and Cox's Downs stations, the first in 1947, and the last in the 1990s. The second was built after the first one kept filling up with shingle and blocking the water during storms, of which there were many. As Donald intended, Mount

ABOVE An old notice in the woolshed. BINNIE FAMILY COLLECTION
OPPOSITE The old dairy and cool room. MARY HOBBS

Cook Station was independent of power companies for many decades, but in recent years has taken its power from the national grid.

One winter day Ray Binnie, who was Donald's right-hand man on the property, was clearing shingle from the entrance to the power plant when a boulder rolled onto his foot and trapped him in the middle of the river. A nor'west storm was forecast, which could rapidly raise the water level, turning the river into a raging torrent. After trying to dislodge the great rock that held him, Ray lay cold and exhausted from his efforts. Donald became alarmed when, later on, Ray did not turn up, and the police and neighbours were called in to help search. At 9 p.m. Hamish Mackenzie found Ray where he and his father Duncan suspected he might be and managed to roll the boulder off him.

Donald also applied his engineering skills to overcome the inconvenience of opening gates for cattle in his yards. He could stand at a console and, from a distance, direct the opening and closing of the various gates, by compressed air.

He had remarkable success as a breeder of high-quality merinos, regularly achieving top sales for wool sent to England. Donald even fed selected merino stock by hand and covered them with canvas jackets. In 2000 his dedication paid off when, in a competition started by luxury Italian textile and clothing company Loro Piana, he set a world record for the finest wool in a full bale. Donald's wool was 13.1 microns – the measurement of the diameter of a wool fibre: the lower the figure, the finer the wool. Loro Piana paid over $120,000 for a 100-kilogram bale of Mount Cook Station fleece.[20]

It has been said that age was just a number to Donald and that seems true enough, as he summited Nun's Veil (2743 metres) on his seventieth birthday with a couple of friends. When the editor of Country-Wide Southern rang Donald, then in his eighties, late one night he was told that he was out rabbit shooting and not expected back for several hours. After deciding to retire, Donald disposed of his sheep but missed them so much that he started a new sheep-breeding programme when he was in his nineties. At that age he was still driving his trusty Land Rover.

Donald relied on men like Ray Binnie who, with his wife Maureen, worked loyally on the station for many years. Ray found it very upsetting to dispose of finely crafted old huts and many artefacts of great historical and sentimental value, which Donald ordered destroyed in his later years. He either no longer had a use for them or was perhaps concerned others might not care for them.

Donald never married. He lived on the station with his sister Catriona, who married later in life. Neither sibling had children. They set up a charitable trust that benefits specific charities they were keen to help. Anyone visiting the station in the later years of Donald's life would have seen a man who was clearly the descendant of Scots Highlanders, proudly wearing a tartan tie. In 2010, aged 95, he fell and fractured his hip and later died in Timaru Hospital. At the time of his death he was still working the land he loved, searching for his sheep, who always came to see what he had brought for them.

The diminutive, but dignified woman opened the gate and stepped inside the paddock. She held a small stick. Two huge bulls were pawing the ground, spoiling for a fight. Walking purposefully towards them, she raised the stick slightly and said firmly, 'That will do!' The bulls obediently stopped pawing the ground.

Catriona St Barbe Baker, daughter of T.D. Burnett and sister to Donald, was decisive, firm, to the point and made no fuss. Her authority did not end with bulls: she was able to split up fighting sheepdogs and her talent with horses was renowned. Because her father was an MP, Catriona was exposed to politics from an early age and was always interested in it, but her heart lay at Mount Cook Station, so she remained there. She also inherited Balmoral and Cox's Downs stations after her father died. Balmoral was later sold and Cox's Downs is now part of Mount Cook.

As an expert rider, Catriona regularly joined the men on musters; in later years she drove the Land Rover. The fine, clear air, the wide open spaces and riding were all things she loved, but sometimes accidents happened. Lifelong family friend Maureen Vance arrived at the station one day to find that Donald had fitted a half-boot stirrup to each saddle. Catriona's horse had suddenly taken fright and bolted. As she had fallen, her foot had become caught in the stirrup and the horse had dragged her, with her head bouncing along on the ground. The animal had eventually

been halted, but Catriona had been lucky to survive. Her brother was so alarmed that he took steps to ensure it would never happen again: after the accident, half-boot stirrups were used by everyone on the station.

In the early days, the coach to the Hermitage would drop the mail for Mount Cook Station at Glentanner, and Catriona would ride across the Tasman River to collect it, wending her way over countless channels and back again, expertly avoiding quicksands and dangerous currents. Young Graeme Murray from Tekapo thought this looked pretty easy so had a go, but was only part-way over the first stream when he nearly drowned. He quickly gained new respect for this woman of the hills.

In 1953 Catriona's life took an unexpected turn. She and her mother were in Dunedin to attend a reception held by the owner of Glenfalloch in honour of Englishman, Richard St Barbe Baker, who had created a foundation, Men of the Trees, to encourage the world to plant more trees. Several years later Catriona travelled to Europe with an aunt and they met Richard again at the home of a mutual friend.

Richard visited Mount Cook Station the following year, and he thoroughly enjoyed himself. As he recounts in his book, *My Life, My Trees*, after he left he felt that something was missing. He soon realised that it was Catriona. He wrote her a letter asking her to marry him and advising he would call at 10 a.m. the following Monday to get her answer. The call was long distance and the last 50 kilometres of the phone system was on a single line. On that particular Monday there was a great nor'west storm, which caused strong interference on the line. He found himself shouting his proposal down the phone. He could barely hear Catriona shouting back, 'Yes!' She was later struck by the irony that for most of the summer Richard had been at the station, where there were any number of idyllic locations to go down on bended knee.

They were married on 7 October 1959 at St David's Pioneer Memorial Church in Cave – Catriona was the first Burnett to be wed there. Richard recalled the little town as being 'astir in anticipation of the wedding'.[21] Catriona was driven from Mount Cook Station to the church, which could hold only 100 of the several hundred guests. A large marquee was erected at the Burnett family home at Aorangi, Cave, for the reception and the wedding cake was balanced on top of a western red cedar that was to be planted beside the local Sunday school that Catriona had built in memory of her mother. Catriona later described hers as a 'tree wedding' as 'guests brought their choice of tree written on a card and the trees were then delivered and planted at a later date'.[22]

The couple enjoyed a brief honeymoon on Stewart Island, before, back at the station, Catriona was pressed into service helping with the mustering and shearing. The house was expanded to include Richard's 30 cases of books, as well as his files and records. Mount Cook Station became Richard's headquarters for his work with trees and for a project he initiated in the Sahara to reclaim land from the desert. He travelled extensively, spending his summers at the station with Catriona and the New Zealand winter in the northern hemisphere. Catriona appears to have joined him overseas only once, at a function for the redwood trees, held in California. Richard wrote over 30 books, working from a hut at the station, with splendid views across the valley to the mountains beyond. His son and daughter from a previous marriage visited and they skied at Round Hill and skated at Tekapo.

Catriona worked on the station and helped Richard with his correspondence. When he was home, Richard found time to relax between

writing and gardening. At 74, he completed a horseback ride for charity from the northernmost kauri tree at the top of the North Island to the southernmost kauri tree at the bottom of the South Island. On the way, he spoke at many schools about the importance of planting trees. Richard died in 1982. The Men of the Trees Foundation, now known as the International Tree Foundation, continues his work.

Despite failing eyesight and being bedridden in later years, Catriona dictated several books, including one about her husband and his work. She was very concerned about world pollution but, in an article for the International Tree Foundation, she expressed faith that the 'extraordinary people around the world who are dedicating their lives to saving the planet by halting deforestation, will bring about the change that will save the planet'.[23] Echoing her father, she also urged people to continue with their efforts to plant trees and to protect and care for those they already have.

At 97, Catriona informed several close friends that she would no longer be here the following week. She also mentioned to Ross and Patience Bisset that her body was ready to follow her heart back to the Misty Gorges. She died peacefully, very close to the day she said she would, on 13 November 2014.

With the deaths of Donald and Catriona Burnett, the Burnett family's occupation of Mount Cook Station drew to a close after a century and a half. The property is now managed by Ross and Patience Bisset, who managed the Burnetts' Aorangi property near Cave for 28 years.

As Ray Binnie's wife Maureen once said, 'As you enter the station, it feels as though you've gone back in time by about 30 or 40 years. Time stands still. It feels very special near the old homestead. Peaceful.' The old dairy and cool room are still there, but nothing remains at the site of the first cob cottage, except the remnants of the original orchard, along with cherry plum trees, gargantuan rhododendrons, lime trees, red currants and gooseberries.

For Maureen Vance, who has visited the station regularly since the age of nine, and who first mustered there in 1953–54, 'Going to the station was like coming home. I'll never forget coming down from the top beat on sunset, surrounded by magnificent mountains, with the Tasman Valley beneath, cast in gold. It gives a renewal of spiritual energy. It's calming and peaceful. It is a place where time doesn't really exist.'

BRAEMAR

Mary Murray drove her open car confidently along the 27-kilometre shingle track from Braemar Station, where she lived with her husband George and their family, out towards the Tekapo road. George was driving behind her, but this was not to his satisfaction: he liked to lead. He saw an opportunity to turn the tables at Irishman Creek Bridge. As his wife drove over it he took a shortcut by driving into the stream. Unfortunately his car stalled in the middle and he came to a sudden halt. George saw the fleeting glimpse of a gloved hand giving a royal wave as Mary sped past. She did not stop. George should have known better. After all, he was trying to take on the first woman in the Mackenzie who had driven to Mount Cook.

George was born in 1866 at Greenpark, a small settlement situated about 23 kilometres from Christchurch. Pioneering was in his blood: his mother was from the Gebbie family, who were among the first Europeans to settle in the South Island. In 1843, the Gebbies arrived by boat at Port Cooper from Wellington, with the Deans brothers and the Manson family, aided by Captain Francis Sinclair and John McHutcheson.[1]

In 1894, at the age of 20, George left New Zealand. After spending time in Rhodesia[2] working as a foreman in a diamond mine, he went to Argentina to help manage a sheep and cattle ranch west of Buenos Aires. 'As the Argentine is already one of this colony's most formidable

---

The view across Lake Pukaki from the old shearers' quarters on Braemar Station.
MARY HOBBS

competitors in the London market,' reported the *Press*, 'and is likely to become more so in future, it is just as well that New Zealanders should know as much as possible of the conditions under which the Argentine run-holder works.' George wrote home about the benefits of planting lucerne to fatten stock and commented on the good price received for the seed in Argentina, as long as locusts did not get it and the government did not interfere.[3]

On his return home in the 1890s, via England, George purchased Sawdon Station, just in time to coincide with one of the worst snowstorms in the high country. A great characteristic of pioneers is their ability to innovate and willingness to try something new. In the big snowstorm of 1903, George saved 20,000 sheep by getting them out of the Mackenzie with the new horse-drawn snowplough.[4]

George met the intrepid and courageous Mary Nalder, three years his junior, in Australia, where she was caring for a sick friend.[5] Instead of pursuing a social life of ease, Mary had trained as a nurse in Christchurch under Sibylla Maude, who founded and established the district nursing service that still bears her name. Mary and George married in Christchurch on 27 February 1900. Mary's father, Herbert, bought the

lease of Glenmore Station in 1913 and when he died, five years later, she inherited it and it was farmed by a manager.

George had a fairly impressive record of station ownership in the Mackenzie: after he sold Sawdon in 1903, he purchased Glentanner, which lay north-west of Lake Pukaki, near Mount Cook; in 1905 he bought neighbouring Rhoborough Downs; he sold Rhoborough in 1908 and in 1911 he purchased Braemar, where the Murrays stayed. Mary, who by then had four children, may have had enough of moving and probably wanted to establish a home. In 1913 George sold Glentanner, but Braemar remained in the family until 1957.[6]

William Spotswood Green passed through Braemar in the early 1880s, and described the station in his book, *The High Alps of New Zealand*:

We passed some rich grass land dotted over with good-looking cattle, and passing through a gateway arrived at the station. We drew up at a wooden house where some surveyors were lodging, and as a matter of course we went in and had a feed . . . A vegetable garden and patch of tilled ground adjoined the house; beyond this stood the inevitable galvanized iron wool-shed; then the shepherd's house, and beyond, the brown rolling downs. In the other direction the wide flats of the Tasman River spread themselves away to the foot of the distant hills and the silvery sheen of Lake Pukaki was visible to the southward.[7]

In 1913 George, a respected breeder of merino and Romney sheep, experimented to see whether Angora goats would be profitable, as he was enthusiastic about the high prices paid for mohair fleece. The goats were phased out, so it probably did not work out as well as expected. He also tried Highland cattle and did well with these, although there were some interesting incidents.

When Mary commissioned the talented Timaru photographer, Havelock Williams, to take photos on the station, he saw the cattle near the homestead and thought they would make a great photo on the riverbed. George invited the photographer to accompany him to the river on horseback, after the cattle had been driven down, so Havelock could get closer to his subject. Unfamiliar with riding horses, Havelock gamely

sallied forth and proceeded down to the riverbed where, after some time and still on horseback, he set up the perfect photo. He was ensconced under the dark cloth when he heard a yell, 'Ride for your life!' The Highland bull was heading straight for them, 'head down and with his wicked horns ready for action'. Havelock bravely clung to his mount and, with his camera flying behind him, at last reached the gate. He thought that even George looked a little pale after their wild gallop to escape the vicious horns of the bull. Havelock finally managed to get a photo when the cattle were moved back to the paddock closer to the house, where they had been in the first place.[8] According to the Murray family, the Highland cattle proved difficult to control, so George took them to the Addington saleyards. A few, apparently, had to be shot after they escaped and rampaged out of control.

In 1918, George set up a hydro-generating plant to create power to run farm machinery. They also had enough power to run radiators in every room of the homestead, as well as floodlights for the tennis court. George's great-grandson, John Murray of The Wolds, said that George initially put in a 110-volt system that worked exceptionally well, which was how Braemar came to have power prior to the establishment of the South Canterbury Power Board. George played a large part in the introduction of hydro power at Fairlie.[9]

The harsh climate of the Mackenzie often made its presence felt with very cold winters and destructive snowstorms. In August 1918 George was 'down-country' when bad weather blew up and he and Fred Lance of Glenfield Station (later renamed Ferintosh) immediately decided to return home while they could. They set out on horseback from Fairlie, where 5 centimetres had already fallen, but the snowfall steadily increased: in some parts between Tekapo and Braemar it was a metre deep. After lunch at the Tekapo Hotel at 2.30 p.m. they cut in towards Braemar from Irishman Creek, knowing that they were now only about 13 kilometres from home. Night fell. Progress slowed to a crawl and all signs of the track disappeared. They were lost for several hours. Experienced people in the high country have died in such conditions and the men would have been well aware of their plight.

Finally they struck the creekbed, and eventually came upon a hut that T.D. Burnett had persuaded the Mackenzie County Council to erect for just such situations. 'Never was the sight of a shelter more welcome … the difference between danger and safety.' Although there was no fire, food or bedding, there was a telephone, 'and by this means the travellers were able to relieve the anxiety of their friends'. They 'cheerfully paced the floor till daylight came, and then continued their journey, wet through to the waist.'[10] After departing at 6 p.m., they took another four hours to reach Braemar. Both men were ravenous, as their last meal had been at Tekapo the day before.

The old hut is still there, looking like a Grahame Sydney painting, set in the midst of the bare, vast landscape, under big skies. The old Morse code signals are tacked to the wall, a reminder of how contact was made with surrounding stations. There is no telephone there now, but there are some welcome improvements, including a fireplace and a couple of bunk beds.

In 1919 George took up the issue of settlers being forced to pay an extra fee for their mail to be delivered. He was incensed that the only runholders charged were those on the small side roads. He also wanted better pay for the postmistress. The minister of the day was big on words, strong on commiseration and weak on action, but he did seem to grasp the reality of the situation, since he disclosed that he had been a settler himself. Sounding dangerously like a Monty Python skit, he told George that in his district he had to *build* his own post office, *pay* the postmistress and *lend* a packhorse to carry his mail as well.[11]

A community-minded man, George participated in various A&P shows, especially those at Fairlie and Timaru, and became the chairman of the Mackenzie County Council. The shrubs and trees that line the Fairlie township were planted at his instruction while he was in this role. In the 1920s, he also instigated the Braemar Sports, which were held annually on 26 December for 30 years. George also paid for the land at Lake Tekapo where the famous Church of the Good Shepherd was built.

Mary is fondly remembered by the Murray family. They recall the story of her driving 100 kilometres to Timaru to find a new cook. When she found no one available, she drove to Mays Bakery and asked them to teach her how to bake bread. She then drove straight back to the station

The old Balmoral shelter beside Irishman Creek. MARY HOBBS

and set to work making the meals and baking the bread for a gang of 30 shearers, until the shearing was finished. Jim Murray recalls how his grandmother would get up at 6 a.m. and go to bed at 9 p.m. She also regularly took cold baths.

George and Mary had four children, Bruce, Gerald, Betty and Molly. As their children grew up, a series of family weddings occurred in relatively quick succession. At the time of his marriage to Lulu Hay on 14 September 1925, Bruce was running Godley Peaks, at the head of Lake Tekapo, which his father had bought in 1921. Bruce's sister, Molly, was one of three brides-maids at their wedding, which was the height of 1920s glamour.

> The bride … wore a tubular frock of cream Venetian lace, lined with georgette to tone. The veil, worn over her face, was of line tulle, caught at each side with tiny sprays of orange blossom. Her shoes were of cream and silver tissue, and she carried a cream shower bouquet. The bridesmaids … were dressed alike in pale beige lace frocks, with narrow, rose pink panels back and front. Roses of pink and beige georgette weighted the skirt hems and their beige net scarves were caught with posies of pink and beige.[12]

ABOVE Morse code signals tacked to the wall of the Balmoral shelter. MARY HOBBS
OPPOSITE Looking from the west side of Lake Pukaki towards Braemar. MARY HOBBS

Gerald was the next to marry, to Joyce James of Cave, in September 1929. He had inherited Glenmore Station from his mother two years earlier and he and his wife Joyce made their home there. The property has been in his family ever since.

The ensuing Depression years must have been particularly difficult. After one of the yearly Tekapo Sales, Bruce Hayman, of Tasman Downs Station, remembered George Murray killing sheep on the shores of the lake when they did not sell, because it was cheaper than taking them back to Braemar.

The Mackenzie has been home to an eclectic range of sometimes unexpected people. Among them was Lieutenant-Commander Richard (Dick) Beauchamp, known as Beach, who had commanded a destroyer in the Battle of Jutland during the First World War. After hostilities ended he returned to England, where his wife died soon after giving birth to their daughter. In an attempt to escape his grief he sailed to New Zealand, temporarily leaving his daughter in the care of his mother, and found his way to the Mackenzie, where he worked at Tasman Downs Station and, after some time, met Molly Murray. The couple married at Braemar in February 1930.

According to the *Evening Post*, the guests were received in the billiard room at Braemar, 'which was effectively arranged with vases of orange marigolds, larkspurs, delphiniums, and lupins in shades of blue and backed by feathery greenery'. Molly, who wore honeysuckle brocaded satin, cut the wedding cake with her new husband's sword.[13]

The homestead was beautiful. Caro Murray, who later married Bruce and Lu's older son Michael, remembers the wooden homestead painted in rich white with a green trim. The steps leading up to the front door were quite high. There was a porch over a front door that led to a small sunroom and the top windows were leadlight. Stained timber lined the lower half of the walls inside, which seemed to keep the temperature cooler in summer. As well as the large billiard room, there was a sitting room and a substantial kitchen, which contained a good-sized coal range, and three bedrooms.

After an enormous amount of hard work, gardens were established with rhododendrons, roses, irises, hollyhocks and delphiniums grow-ing in the flower borders. The lawn gently sloped from the house down

towards the river. There was a tennis court, and a swimming pool had been dug out and lined with concrete. At the back of the home there was a large vegetable garden, as well as raspberries and fruit trees. As with all high country stations of this era, there was a dairy and a cool house for butter and cream.

Molly and Beach moved to Tekapo where they built Penscroft, one of the first houses in the village, on a site affording a wonderful view of the lake. The couple had several children and Beach's daughter from his first marriage also came to live with them. Beach took on a station known as the Mount Edward block, east of Lake Tekapo, which proved less than successful. After selling up, they moved back to Braemar for a couple of years. Later, Beach and Molly taught and administered at schools for Maori and underprivileged children.

ABOVE The old Braemar dairy that was relocated before Lake Pukaki was raised. MARY HOBBS
OPPOSITE A rare photo of the old Braemar homestead before Lake Pukaki was raised. MACKENZIE FAMILY COLLECTION

In 1937 Bruce and his wife Lu and their three children, Michael, Rosemary and Tim, moved back to Braemar from Godley Peaks and George and Mary retired to Penscroft, in Tekapo. Although there had been many hard times, George and Mary succeeded in establishing a beautiful home at Braemar and in securing surrounding stations for their two sons. They left a legacy that was rich not only in property, but also in character and fortitude.

In 1939 New Zealand was again plunged into war. Bruce's brother-in-law, Bruce Hay, joined up and left his station, Mount Potts, in the care of Bruce Murray, who was also then running Braemar and Godley Peaks. He sold Godley Peaks to John Scott in 1941. Then George died on 20 November 1943 and the burden of government death duties made expansion plans for the station far more difficult.

It was a struggle for Bruce and Lu, but there were lighter moments, too. Living on a station as remote as Braemar, there was often a problem with the mail. Commercial aviation pioneer Harry Wigley's transport service delivered many of their requirements, but Lu became frustrated when the driver often forgot to drop off their goods at Tekapo and took them all the way to Queenstown. This meant she had to make a second trip over the rough shingle road from Braemar to Tekapo once the goods finally arrived. When there is a gang of contractors to feed in a remote location, all hell can break lose without the essential supplies. However, Harry was a good friend of the Murrays, and the type of person you could easily forgive. On several occasions he would zoom flamboyantly over Braemar in his plane, waggle the wings and drop the day's newspaper in the middle of their front lawn – always dead centre.

Caro Murray remembers Bruce, her father-in-law, as a tease. He was good-humoured and used to enjoy a joke, although it was important not to take his generous nature for granted. He gave a cheque to charity each year. One year, the profit of the station was markedly down, so the cheque was smaller. When the charity collector came he looked at the amount and commented that there seemed to be a mistake. Bruce took the cheque and ripped it up, saying that perhaps the following year they would be happy to receive what they had been given.

Though he was still in his prime years, Bruce's health began to fail. Initially he suffered from an agonisingly painful kidney stone, which required an operation. Despite this, his health deteriorated further and he died in 1950, at the age of 49, just seven years after his father. It was a sad time for the family, made financially tougher by further death duties.

Following Bruce's death, the running of the station was left to trustees, but Michael took over as soon as he was old enough. It was a big job for someone so young. The shearers arrived soon afterwards. Noticing that the sheep were receiving a lot of unnecessary cuts, Michael asked the head shearer to tell his men to be a bit more careful. A few minutes later, the shearer making most of the unnecessary cuts sliced the ear off a sheep. Michael ordered them to down tools and leave. The shearers were incredulous, but Michael stood firm and they packed up, threatening he would be blacklisted. Michael lay awake for most of the night, wondering what the hell he had done and where on earth he would find another gang at such short notice. He rang around the district. New shearers turned up a few days later and the crisis was averted.

Michael had met Caroline (Caro) Cracroft Wilson before his father died. They married at St Barnabas Church in Fendalton, Christchurch in 1951. Caro and her beloved horse then joined Michael on the station. She was well suited to high country life, as she had grown up on a farm that was left from the Cracroft Wilson family estate in Cashmere.

Bruce's widow Lu, her daughter Rosemary and her younger son Tim, remained in the homestead while Michael and Caro refurbished a small cottage, known as Ploughman's, closer to the Tasman River. It had a fireplace in the sitting room, and a coal range in the kitchen, but initially there was no inside toilet. Just before they were married, panic set in, as winter had arrived and the ground was too frozen to dig a hole for the septic tank. So Michael and his brother Tim did what any high country farmer might do when faced with such a predicament: they stuck a piece of dynamite into the soil and lit the fuse. Problem solved. The septic tank and toilet went in.

The cottage required alteration, so Michael contacted his cousin, Miles Warren, later one of New Zealand's most prestigious architects, who had just graduated. He had the front door removed and replaced it with a door of glass. The top half of the door opened independently, which was unheard of in the 1950s. Michael and Caro loved living at Ploughman's Cottage. Sturdy plum trees grew on one side and on the north there was

a shelterbelt to break the prevailing wind. It was their own little spot, set in idyllic surroundings.

It was not long after the war, so there was a shortage of many items. Caro sewed many of their clothes and Lu taught her how to bake and cook. They made sauce, bottled fruit and salted beans and butter. A garden was carved out of the glacial earth with wheelbarrows of boulders removed.

In 1952 Caro became pregnant. Late one night at Braemar, she experienced the unmistakable early signs of labour, even though the baby was not due for six weeks. They phoned Lu to confer, and then set off with a hiss and a roar down the long gravel road from Braemar out to

State Highway 8, to Christchurch, only to run out of petrol at Rakaia. It was past midnight and by this time Caro was well into labour. Rakaia is usually quiet at night, but in 1951 it was positively dead to the world. They eventually managed to wake the local owner of the bowser, as it was called in those days, and he kindly filled the car with fuel. Michael finally drove through the wrought iron gates, under the iron lantern hanging above the entrance to St George's Hospital, and screeched to a halt at the large double doors with the big brass handles. He assisted his wife over the slightly worn front steps, and up into the maternity ward. It was 4.30 a.m.

The night sister came out. 'You can go now,' she told Michael severely, then added over her shoulder, as she led Caro away, 'Don't use the lift.' After obediently creeping down the stairs, Michael found himself back in their car, alone, in the middle of Christchurch, at 5 a.m. He decided to drive to Caro's parents' place, where he had to throw gravel at their bedroom window to wake them. John was born the next day.

By the winter of 1954 Caro was due to have their second baby and Michael was taking no chances. Each day he diligently attended to the road in a vain attempt to keep it open and free of snow between Braemar and State Highway 8, but he was fighting a losing battle so, a month before it was due, Caro went to Christchurch to await the baby's arrival. Susan was born calmly, without the midnight dash. Their third daughter, Tessa, was born in 1959.

After two lots of crippling death duties within a decade, the Murray family came to the sad conclusion that Braemar, their home since 1911, would have to be sold. There was insufficient finance to be able to keep them all on the station and have enough to invest in the property, too. Caro and Michael moved to The Wolds, Tim went to Maryburn Station, Rosemary built a house at Glengyle, near Mount Somers, and Lu eventually shifted to a house in Christchurch.

～

In 1957, the New Zealand and Australian Land Company Ltd purchased the station as a going concern and retained ownership until 1968, when Braemar was sold to the Studholmes. In 1969, Duncan Mackenzie purchased a half-share, and in 1975 Duncan and his wife Carol took full ownership.

Duncan and Carol had met in 1968, at a Young Farmers' and Country Girls' Club stock-judging event in Nelson. Both had grown up on farms, Duncan on 1000 hectares at Waihaorunga, west of Waimate, and Carol on Pine Farm, near Oxford, North Canterbury, a 320-hectare Aberdeen Angus and Corriedale sheep stud. They married at Pine Farm in November 1969 and moved to Braemar the following January.

Within two years they had a daughter, Annabel. The year after her arrival, the district was engulfed by a substantial snowfall. Over 60 centimetres of snow settled at Braemar, so a lot of snow-raking had to be done to give the sheep a fighting chance. There was not much of a breather for Duncan and Carol before their son Hamish was born. Those early years were incredibly busy.

Even in the 1970s, Braemar remained remote. The road between the station and State Highway 8 was still rough, so travelling was kept to a minimum, which, with winter snowstorms, increased the sense of isolation. Tekapo, the closest village, had only a hotel, a store and a petrol pump. A journey to Timaru or Oamaru was required for farm implements, or to see stock firms. Carol taught the children through Correspondence School.

The Mackenzies bravely purchased the station on the eve of one of the most tumultuous times in its history as, six years later, work for the second raising of Lake Pukaki began. The homestead, most farm buildings, the yards and shelter, and 400 hectares of Braemar disappeared under water when the lake was raised another 38 metres. The compensation paid did not come close to what was lost. Part of the problem was that the government was trying to apply an old policy that compensated for railway tracks across land, but did not take into account lost buildings, yards, power plants, shelterbelts, fences and other facilities. Nor did it consider the negative effect on the station as a unit when a percentage of the most productive land – 25 per cent in Braemar's case – was removed. The legal term for it is 'injurious affection'. After a fair bit of robust discussion back and forth, the Mackenzies took the Ministry of Works to

Duncan Mackenzie musters sheep in the early 1970s. MACKENZIE FAMILY COLLECTION

court. (They were the only station holders to do so.) It was a long drawn-out, harrowing battle but Duncan and Carol emerged triumphant and received almost double the amount the ministry was originally prepared to pay. The time and stress took a toll, however, and there were legal fees to cover.

As this was being settled, Duncan and Carol were under pressure to build a new house, rebuild the yards and farm buildings and keep the station viable. They moved many of the old buildings, including a hayshed, a classic barn that had been imported from Scotland, as well as a concrete dairy, originally sited at the back of the old homestead, a storeshed, a woolshed, some of the shearers' quarters and an old schoolhouse, where the Murray children had done their Correspondence lessons. They were all fine buildings, most of them made by George Murray of sound rimu, on which he insisted. Good-quality galvanised pipe was saved from under the old house, as well as a mantelpiece from the dining room, which remains in use as an antique bedhead for Duncan and Carol. Mary's beautiful gardens were submerged, along with hundreds of trees that the Murrays had planted. Duncan and Carol had to re-establish Braemar from scratch, on bare land.

In 1996 Duncan switched to Perendales, a move unheard of in the heart of merino country. He made the change because the merinos on Braemar were prone to footrot, owing to more rainfall, browntop and fescue, and little in the way of stony country on the freehold area. Footrot is less common on stony land where the soil drains more freely. What they lost in wool income was balanced by the Perendales' fat lambs. Duncan and his staff put in a lot of fencing, improved the pastures and rebuilt the homestead and other sheds. He also subdivided the land into more paddocks on the low country. Duncan increased mustering into more remote areas of the station and reminisces fondly about the camaraderie of those days.

After almost 38 years on the station, Duncan and Carol retired from Braemar in 2007. They now live near Timaru, close to where their daughter Annabel lives with her partner Bryce Gibson, also a farmer, and their two children, Dougal and Oscar. Back at Braemar, the outstanding gardens and trees at the station stand as testimony to the enormous effort and love they have put into this land for future generations.

Hamish Mackenzie, known as Mish, who had worked on Braemar with his father, took over completely in 2007. His wife, Julia, grew up on Glenfalloch Station at the head of the Rakaia Valley, so was well versed in high country life. The couple has two children, Kate and Gus. Initially the family lived in an older cottage on Braemar while renovations were made to the main house.

Things were progressing well until Mish went on a hunting trip with Ben Innes from Black Forest Station and the helicopter crashed. Mish managed to walk out unaided, but immediately had the feeling that something was terribly wrong. He lay down and did not get up again for four weeks. He was admitted to Christchurch Hospital and then transferred to Burwood,

ABOVE Hamish (Mish) and Julia Mackenzie with their children, Gus and Kate. MARY HOBBS
OPPOSITE Shepherd Harry Railton moves sheep in late summer. MARY HOBBS

where he had operations to stabilise several fractures of his lumbar vertebrae. After several months of recuperation he made a full recovery.

While Mish was in hospital Julia was at Braemar with two toddlers and just a couple of shepherds, so Duncan came back to help with the running of the station. The house renovations were incomplete. On one particularly cold morning, when Julia went over to the house with the carpet layer to measure up for a small piece that was to be replaced, she found the pipes had burst. Calf-deep in water that was still gushing out, she had no idea where to turn it off. She called Duncan. Within minutes he directed her to the right spot. The carpet layer looked on. 'So, I should measure up for the whole house now?' he asked.

Despite the frantic schedule and the long drive, Julia still regularly made it down to Burwood Hospital to visit her husband, who was finding the experience there very humbling. Some of his fellow patients were not able to move from the neck down, yet, with each step of progress he made, they were among the most encouraging of all.

A couple of years ago there was a tussle with a bull that ended with

Mish falling into an electric fence and sustaining a compound fracture of his ulna. He was soon back at work, however, and since then has been accident-free and life on the station now has an ordered feel to it. After a tremendous amount of work, there has been a diversification into tourism with the old shearers' quarters and various other cottages on the station turned into accommodation for visitors, including those on the Alps 2 Ocean Cycle Trail, which goes straight past their gate.

The Mackenzies love it here. There is nowhere else they would rather be. 'Nothing is short term,' says Julia. 'We never intend to sell, so it's not about the next ten years for us, it's about our lifetime. We love sharing Braemar with others. We love it when they enjoy it. The views change all the time, and we often say, "Hey, look at Cook in that light." We feel very, very, blessed to be able to live here. Neither of us takes it for granted.'

ABOVE Aoraki/Mt Cook in early morning sun, as cyclists on the Alps 2 Ocean Trail prepare to depart Braemar. MARY HOBBS
OPPOSITE Charlie Hobbs cycles out from Braemar Station. MARY HOBBS
OVERLEAF Mist rolls up the lake towards Braemar. MARY HOBBS

TASMAN DOWNS

In 1920, Walter Hayman asked his son Jack to go and look after Tasman Downs Station until he could sell it. 'Johnnie, my boy, you had better go up and look after the godforsaken place till we can get rid of the bloody thing!'[1] The Hayman family is still there.

Their story began with Tom Hayman and Ann Kingsbury, who married in England in 1859 and made their way to Australia in 1862 with two young sons, Frederick and Walter. Ann gave birth to their third son, John, en route. The young family met with bad luck in Australia when their home was burned down over an argument about a waterhole. Ann and the children barely escaped with their lives. Tom was away at the time, but when he returned he immediately packed up the family and moved to New Zealand. They arrived in Lyttelton in March 1865, with little more than the clothes they stood up in. They made their way to Ann's brother's home near Leithfield, where Tom found a job driving the first lot of cattle to the West Coast.

In 1867 they moved to Cust, in North Canterbury, where they built a sod cottage on the small farm they had bought, and in 1877 purchased 250 acres at Willowby, close to Ashburton. By this time they had 12 children. Between the ages of 20 and 45, Ann gave birth to 18 children, one of whom was stillborn. Sadly, Ann died of peritonitis, six years after the birth of her last child, aged 51.

In his entertaining autobiography, *The Nut that Changed My Life*, her

---

Hayman's Road, and the entrance to Tasman Downs. MARY HOBBS

great-grandson Bruce Hayman pays tribute to 'Ann the beloved', who was 'almost worshipped' by her family and 'made time to befriend, counsel and care for neighbours and all who needed help'.[2]

Tom and Ann's son Walter, and his wife Elizabeth (née Frampton), farmed in the Ashburton area from 1883 to 1896, when they won a land ballot and purchased a 360-acre farm in South Canterbury, named Opiro.

Tasman Downs was originally part of Balmoral Station. After several earlier owners, it was purchased by Mr Schlaepfer, who owned the station from 1900 to 1914. Walter bought Tasman Downs Station from Herbert Elworthy in 1915, in the belief that the dry high country air might help his 23-year-old daughter Daisy overcome tuberculosis. But at Fairlie, on her way to Tasman Downs, she deteriorated and was taken back to the hospital at Waipiata in Central Otago, where she died.

Walter's son John (Jack) Hayman and his wife Lilian (née Griffin) lived and worked at Opiro for five years. By 1919 they had two daughters, three-year-old Patricia Daisy, and Elizabeth de Carteret, known as

Betty, who was born on 16 September 1917. Their only son, Bruce, was due near Christmas of 1919. All was going well until Patricia died from peritonitis on 7 December. Bruce was born just a few weeks afterwards, on 26 December. It was several months after this that Walter asked Jack to go up and look after Tasman Downs until he could sell it. Still grieving for their daughter, Jack and Lilian may well have looked upon the station as a fresh start. And indeed it was.

The couple arrived in July 1920, with baby Bruce and Betty. The manager had resigned and the buildings were very basic. There was a small shearing shed, a chaff shed, a stable and a small tack room for horse harness. The 'house' consisted of a kitchen and bedroom. There was no electricity. There were also a couple of mobile huts, as well as a lean-to. Water came from a spring about 100 metres from the house and had to be carried over by bucket.

Tasman Downs is remote. Subdivided from Balmoral Station in 1878, it lies on the east side of Lake Pukaki, south of Braemar. It had four owners before Walter Hayman. In the early 1900s, Tasman Downs was roughly 830 hectares in size, modest compared with other stations in the district, which averaged around 10,000 hectares or more. It was 30 kilometres over a rough shingle road from the Tekapo Hotel, where papers and mail were delivered, over 70 kilometres from Fairlie and 135 kilometres from Timaru. Petrol was expensive; cars were rare.

It was early spring when Bruce, aged three, suffered from a serious ear infection and soaring temperature. The roads were completely blocked by snow and the temperature outside had plummeted to minus 17°C. After several motor failures trying to get to Tekapo, they finally made it late that afternoon, thanks to Jack's ability to fix motors. It had taken them eight hours to travel 30 kilometres. It took two more hours to get to Fairlie, where a surgeon met them. A mastoid operation was immediately performed and Bruce's life was saved.

Despite the obstacles, Jack and Lilian bravely settled in and made a home. Several children lived on other high country stations in the area, so Lilian, who had attended Canterbury College with Daisy Hayman from about 1908 and received teacher training, turned the old tack room into a school for her children, as well as those from Braemar and Guide Hill and others wanting to attend. When it opened on 6 February 1923 there were nine children on the roll. The Education Board helped to furnish the school, but a lot of work was needed to get the old room serviceable. Lilian later also took on school boarders. Many children were sent to Tasman Downs from all over the country to improve their health in the dry high country air; at times there was a waiting list of 50. They would arrive wheezing with various respiratory complaints and return home rosy-cheeked and full of energy. Day pupils rode to school on horseback, while boarders stayed in accommodation on the station.

High country life suited young Bruce. He swam, shot rabbits, tickled trout, and enjoyed ice skating and tobogganing. Later on he joined the local ice hockey team and, despite severe winter temperatures, never missed a practice or match. Like his father and grandfather, whose imaginations seemed unlimited and were put to good use on the station, Bruce was great at creating things. By the age of 10, he was adept at using tin snips, a soldering iron and rivets to make what he needed from materials at hand. Old kerosene tins and their packing cases were transformed into handy boxes, small drawers, shelves, sledges, go-karts, rabbit hutches or tree houses. The main ingredients were access to a workshop and an active imagination.

In 1932 it was arranged that 12-year-old Bruce would spend part of the school holidays with a friend in Christchurch. He had the opportunity of going by bus to Fairlie and then catching a train to Christchurch, or he could ride with Bill Hamilton from Irishman Creek in his Bentley, brought back from Britain. As Bruce recalled, 'Naturally I chose the ride in the Bentley. What boy wouldn't!'[3]

Bill did not dally. Despite the roads being of rough shingle, he hardly ever drove anywhere under 110 kilometres an hour. On the one small 18-kilometre section of seal, between Rolleston and Christchurch, Bill reached speeds of 160 kilometres an hour. No seatbelts in those days. Hair blown back, bodies braced against the seats, they were gripped by the exhilarating thrill of adventure.

During the holidays, Bruce and his friend Paddy Davis were never idle. They put a tremendous amount of effort into building a boat with a motor made from materials to hand. After painstakingly fixing faults, they eventually got it mobile and trialled it on the Avon River. Traffic ground to a halt as drivers and passengers gaped at the sight. Their photo appeared in the paper with a report on their achievement.

Making a Motor Boat

My friend Paddy Davis, who lives near the Avon, in Christchurch, built a flat bottom boat. For a long time, he was satisfied with this, then he thought he would like to have an engine in it, so he put an advertisement in the paper for a motor bicycle engine. He received one answer, that sounded well, so he went round to see the man, who said he could have the whole bicycle, for £1. Paddy was very pleased at this, and the next day the man rode it round to his place at Avonside. It had a practically new tyre on the front wheel, and the rear

After two-and-a-half years at Timaru Boys' High School, Bruce persuaded his parents to allow him to leave and help his father on the farm. They agreed and Bruce happily returned home in 1935, but working on the station did not stop him from taking the odd holiday, one of which was a two-week camping trip to Queenstown in 1939, on his 1918 Harley-Davidson.

In November 1938, tragedy struck the family again. Bruce's sister Betty, who had just completed training as a teacher in Dunedin, died of spinal meningitis. She was only 21 years old.

～

Any free days would usually find Bruce indulging in his favourite pastimes, including polo, which was held within a 16-kilometre radius of

ABOVE Bruce Hayman during pilot training in World War II. HAYMAN FAMILY COLLECTION
OPPOSITE A joyous welcome home: Bruce Hayman with his parents on his return from the war. HAYMAN FAMILY COLLECTION

Tekapo. He ferried horses to the polo matches by riding a horse and leading others. The players of the 1930s read like a who's who of some of the early high country stations, and included Bruce Murray from Godley Peaks, Gerald Murray from Glenmore, Bill Hamilton from Irishman Creek, Ron Hoskins from Simons Hill and Charlie Parker and his son, Tim, from Halbrook.

Bruce had a horse called Lady Gay, on which he particularly enjoyed playing polo. She became so used to the game that if she spotted a mushroom, or something similar while on the station, thinking it was a ball she would position herself where Bruce could get a good shot at it. If he missed she would turn around so he could have another crack. Although good with polo, she was very skittish around water, so was of no use when mustering on the low-lying land at the head of Lake Pukaki and out across the braided streams of the Tasman River. Bruce did not relish working in this area but this 200 hectares of river flats and islands were an important part of the station. Because it was warmer, stock could graze there when the rest of the property was under snow. The downside was that if a storm blew up they had to move the stock quickly, and on one occasion 300 sheep were lost in a flash flood.

Bruce's next horse, Pinto, had no fear of water and probably saved his life from quicksands situated near the Tasman River. Although Bruce did his best to avoid dodgy areas by testing them out with a mustering stick, there were a few occasions when he got it wrong. Several times he urged Pinto forward, while attempting to get sheep out of the area before an impending nor'west storm, and she would refuse to budge and inevitably choose another area that turned out to be much safer.

When war was declared in September 1939 Bruce did not volunteer, as he was needed on the farm, and when the army did call him up, his parents successfully appealed, so he spent about a year as part of the Home Guard. But Bruce did not feel he was doing all he could. 'So on the first working day in January 1941, when I had just turned 21, I hopped on the Harley and off down to the Recruiting Office in Timaru and offered my services to the Royal New Zealand Air Force, hoping to be a pilot.'[4] It's not difficult to imagine how his parents felt. Having already lost two of their three children, the prospect of their only son going to war on the other side of the world must have been a nightmare.

After being 'knocked into shape at Levin',[5] Bruce and his fellow recruits were split up and sent to various places for flight training – for Bruce it was Harewood in Christchurch. Then came more training in Saskatchewan, Canada, under the British Commonwealth Air Training Plan. With a total of 230 flying hours under his belt, Bruce headed east for leave in New York and then crossed the Atlantic for operational training in England.

Bruce's adventures at war were many and varied – he flew in the Middle East, North Africa and Europe – but the one constant through them all is how he applied the creative skills he learned on a high country station in one of the most remote parts of New Zealand. A great example of this was when Bruce and his crew were stuck in North Africa waiting with hundreds of other men for aircraft. The noncommissioned officers were given a couple of blankets and a shared tent as accommodation. It was uncomfortable, so the Anzacs created a better solution: they found aluminium framing from a wrecked aircraft, quite a few old 225-kilogram bomb cartons and metres of discarded telephone wire. From this they constructed beds with wire bases. It was not the Hilton but it gave them a much better sleep.

The crew had to practise flying drills, but one beautiful day, as they flew over a deserted beach, they all decided a swim would help to boost morale. What could be better? Bruce landed the plane on the beach, they all had a swim, then the tide came in and they had to frantically fight against time to dig the wheels of the plane out of the sand before they were swamped.

Bruce was also invaluable when it came to adding a bit of fresh meat to the diet to liven up the boring dehydrated food. When the rest of the team discovered he used to kill, skin and dress a sheep every week back home, they went on a sortie to find a likely prospect. Bruce honed the kitchen knife with a roadside stone, killed the sheep, took the skin off and had the innards out in short order. Everyone enjoyed a hearty meal that night.

Bruce and his crew flew many operations in Europe. Every flight was dangerous and carried the risk that they might not return. They admirably kept their nerve, but their luck ran out when, in December 1943, their Wellington bomber crashed into the side of the 10,000-foot Mount Etna in Italy, owing to bad weather and a navigational error. One of the crew was killed instantly, aviation fuel was leaking under the plane, and

Bruce felt as though he was floating and wondered if he was already dead. When he looked back he saw he was sitting in the seat, but seemed to have moved forward. He guessed he was still alive but he found it difficult to do anything to save himself because he could not feel his body. A finger had been stripped of flesh and nail, and was spraying blood with each beat of his heart. His jaw was injured, his left leg was stripped of a chunk of muscle and tendon and he had a compound fracture of his tibia and fibula. He managed to crawl around 20 metres from the plane, at about 2740 metres up Mount Etna.

Next day, despite a fractured jaw and other injuries, two other crew members made their way down the mountain. Another died. Now there was just Bruce left on site with the plane, along with one other crew member with a spinal injury. By the third day Bruce felt like dozing off, but knowing that would be fatal, forced himself to stay awake by reciting stories and as much poetry as he could remember.

Then he heard a couple of rifle shots, which heralded the arrival of the leader of the Sicilian Mafia and two other members. At this point Bruce had the presence of mind to fish out a card he had been issued with, promising that if he was found and rescued, the rescuer would be paid £1000. The guns were put away, the whisky came out and Bruce and his mate were carried down the mountain and, by some miracle, survived. That was the end of the war for Bruce.

While convalescing in England, he met and married a British girl named Toni. After a short honeymoon Bruce was sent back to New Zealand, without his new bride, arriving in mid-1945. He remembered a very happy, musical return on a troopship with other servicemen, including many from the Maori Battalion. A heavy snowfall made it a slow rail journey from Christchurch to Timaru, where his relieved and delighted parents were waiting to meet him. Although he continued to be plagued by the injuries to his leg, Bruce got straight back into farm work. He put his name down to win a ballot, for returned servicemen, for a farm on government land, but his name never came up.

In 1946, Toni, along with many other war brides, arrived in New Zealand to begin a new life with Bruce on Tasman Downs. Between 1946 and 1954, Bruce and Toni had four children: Alan, Bernard, Nicola and Wendy.

When his parents retired in 1952, and Bruce took over the running of the station, he thought the Government Rehabilitation Loans Board would give him financial assistance through a lower interest rate on a loan, as was provided for returned servicemen after the war. He was shocked to be refused. 'When told [the property] was on the shores of Lake Pukaki, they simply replied that no money was available for any properties in the Mackenzie, as no land up there was economic.'[6] After putting his life on the line for his country, fulfilling all that was required of him and returning with a leg that gave him constant pain and little movement, it was a crushing blow. To make matters worse, the government had begun raising the lake for the hydro-electric power scheme and 200 hectares had already disappeared. By the time the work was completed, the station had lost almost 300 hectares of prime land.

Bruce supplemented the family income with contract haymaking and harvesting work for neighbours from Braemar and Guide Hill and worked all the hours he had to make a go of it. On 14 June 1961 he returned from a trip to Fairlie to find the house 'strangely quiet'. The governess who had been helping Bruce and Toni's daughters with their correspondence broke the news that Toni had left and moved to Christchurch with Nicola (10) and Wendy (seven). Bruce later found a note from Toni that said she was leaving with the girls and he could have the boys. Fourteen-year-old Alan and 12-year-old Bernard were boarders at Timaru Boys' High School. 'To say I was shattered,' wrote Bruce many years later, 'would be the understatement of the year.'[7]

With his neighbour John Hogg from Guide Hill happy to look after the property, he headed for Christchurch to find his family and talk to his daughters. But while he was away gale-force winds suddenly hit the high country. Sparks from a dying fire were blown into the hayshed which, with 2000 bales of winter feed, was reduced to ashes. The old chaff house and stable, which included the old schoolroom, were also burnt. The farm implements housed in the stable, including the header, baler, top-dresser and chaff-cutter were all gone. None of it was insured.

For a moment Bruce was tempted to give up, but decided he was not about to leave. 'In spite of my war injuries classing me as 75% disabled, I was determined to prove to the bloody bureaucrats that this bit of God's Earth had been worth fighting for.'[8] He comforted himself that the house, his workshop, the toolshed and the garage were still there and the car, tractor and a 4-ton truck had not been damaged.

The community rallied. They helped to clear up after the fire and those who attended the goose drive fundraiser collected £500 to enable a very grateful Bruce to purchase another header, which helped him to get back on his feet. The following year Tasman Downs went onto the national grid with electric power, but this 'most wonderful event' meant a lot of modifications to the house, which Bruce did himself. He also built a new storeroom and sheds. Before the power was turned on, the private phone line that had been owned by Mount Cook Station, Braemar, Tasman Downs and Guide Hill, needed to be upgraded. John from Guide Hill and Bruce did a great deal of work to get the new telegraph poles ready. Donald Burnett from Mount Cook Station also worked on the project. Bruce said he hoped it would last for another 50 years; Donald preferred it to be 100. As it turned out, the digital world took over 25 years later.

After Toni and the girls left, Bruce's widowed mother came up to help but extra assistance was needed when the boys were home on holiday. Linda Cargo, who was working as a governess at Haldon Station, agreed to help out temporarily. Fate intervened, however, and Linda and Bruce were married in 1963. They had two children, Jane (in 1967) and Ian (in

The view south down Lake Pukaki from Tasman Downs. MARY HOBBS

80

1971). So the fortune-teller in the East whom Bruce had consulted for a lark during the war had ultimately proved to be correct: he had told Bruce he would have four or six children.

Life was happy and fulfilling for Linda and Bruce, but they still faced challenges. In the mid 1970s Lake Pukaki was raised for the final time, which reduced the station to just over 500 hectares and necessitated rebuilding their home on higher land. The government offer to do this was much too low and there were endless visits to lawyers in an attempt to achieve compensation at market value.

Bruce's response was to go into the timber business, cutting down Oregon trees on the property to provide the timber required for the new house. Cut at a local sawmill, the timber was brought back to the station to season for 18 months. The house took two years to build and in that time Bruce cut logs, drew plans and mixed concrete. He and Linda hand-collected 56 tonnes of local rocks for the exterior, carted them, and supervised the Ministry of Works moving farm buildings from the lake edge to higher ground. Bruce also did the plumbing and the steel reinforcing required for this high-wind area. 'Thank goodness that at the time, I was a young fellow of only 55.'[9]

In 1982 Linda and Bruce started up a homestay, which attracted visitors from all over the world who enjoyed a unique experience and warm country hospitality at Tasman Downs. Although very active, Bruce continued to have a lot of trouble with his leg and eventually had it amputated, which left him free of pain and constant hospital stays for skin grafts. Work on the farm gradually changed from sheep to cattle – the last sheep left the station in 1996 – and some cropping is still done. Bruce kept busy all his life, but he and Linda still found the time to have enormous fun jet boating in the South Island. Of Bruce's children from his first marriage, Wendy and her family live in Christchurch, and Alan and Bernard live in South Canterbury. Nicola died as a young wife and mother. Linda and Bruce's daughter, Jane, part-owns a farm near Ashburton. She has two children, Thomas and Mary. Ian runs Tasman Downs and lives there with his wife, Nicky, and their son, Archie.

Bruce died in May 2008 but Linda, who is fit and active, with a sharp mind and a ready sense of humour, still lives at the station and the homestay is still open. Her imprint is also big on this land.

Riders on the Alps 2 Ocean Cycle Trail who pass Tasman Downs, by the beautiful lake, see that the paddocks are all named. One, bearing the title of Bruce's book, was made by Ian as a tribute to his father.

Ian Hayman is clearly one of a kind, from the hat perched on top of his unruly hair, to part of an old phone, complete with spiral cord, attached to a cell phone in his breast pocket. He wears a formal old jacket over shirt and frayed denim shorts or jeans.

When he was nominated as the local fundraiser to obtain money for a new MRI scanner in Timaru Hospital he toured the district raising funds with a spare leg of his father's for people to pop donations into. He also auctioned meat at a local farmers' day, and then auctioned himself, dressed in a 'mankini', miming the actions of window cleaning, sweeping and other household chores, just so the audience did not get the wrong idea about what he was selling, even if it was to the song, 'I'm Sexy and I Know It'. Ian raised around $7500.

ABOVE Linda Hayman at Tasman Downs. MARY HOBBS
OPPOSITE Bruce Hayman sits with young Gus Mackenzie as the mist rolls up the lake. JOHN BISSET COLLECTION

On a drive around the station people are introduced to his main helper, Robert, a benign presence often found keeping guard in the yards, sitting on a chair by an old caravan, wine bottle in hand, sunglasses on. A bicycle rests against a post nearby. He does not speak as he surveys his domain. The reason for the silence is that Robert is a mannequin.

Once Robert was seated in a deckchair on the road just outside the gate, a bottle of Speight's in hand and holding a toy gun, in an attempt to slow down the lorries travelling down the shingle road, which were kicking up dust for kilometres. When Christine, a friend of Linda's, sat on Robert's knee in a bikini giving him a kiss, the trucks rapidly slowed and nearly drove off the road. And when film-maker Sir Peter Jackson and his crew of hundreds descended on Tasman Downs to build Lake-Town on the shore of Pukaki for *The Hobbit: The Desolation of Smaug*, Robert had the uncanny knack of popping up in Portaloos, at security-guard posts, at lunch, keeping an eye on things.

ABOVE Robert keeps guard. MARY HOBBS
OPPOSITE Ian Hayman harvesting at Tasman Downs, with Aoraki/Mt Cook in the distance. MARY HOBBS

When a reporter came to interview Ian, Robert was 'welding' in the shed. To be precise, the welding machine was on and Robert, with protective visor and wig, was bent over the machine. Asked where he got all his ideas from, Ian nodded towards Robert, saying he was the main ideas man. Understandably, the reporter wanted to talk to Robert.

'Robert,' Ian called out. 'Robert! *Robert!*'

'Is he a bit deaf?' asked the reporter.

'Yes, but still, there's no excuse for that!' Ian exclaimed, as he strode over to Robert and pulled his hair off.

The reporter shrieked in alarm, accompanied by a few apt expletives, until she realised the truth.

Ian employs his creative skills wherever he sees a use for them and now passes his knowledge on to his son Archie. He enjoys taking tourists on farm tours, telling them the family stories and showing them the historical areas and the places where scenes from *The Hobbit* were filmed. A born entertainer with a wide repertoire of great tales, he is a natural at this job.

Yet behind all the fun is a talented farmer, metal-worker, artist, entertainer, farm tour operator, respecter of history, family man, husband and

father, with a keen sense of the importance of looking after the land. Ian is the fourth in a line of farmers and creators who have handed down the gift of their skills and knowledge to the next generation. The station has many examples of the Haymans' talents. Old post drivers were made, grader blades and even a miniature steam-powered tractor, built by Jack in the early 1900s. It still works. A roof on the fertiliser shed winds up so trucks do not have to shovel out, but can just dump directly. Bruce made a gravity-fed water pump with a wooden waterwheel to supply water to the homestead. A piece of 4" x 2" in the shed has been fashioned into an International M tractor, complete with trailer, made to scale from found materials. When Bruce and Linda's daughter Jane became engaged, Linda thought it would be nice to hold the wedding in one of the picturesque high country churches, but Jane wanted to get married at Tasman Downs. Bruce solved the problem by building a lattice church in their backyard, with a view of Aoraki/Mt Cook. It was the perfect solution. It still stands, with the old schoolhouse bell given new life in the steeple.

When it came to dealing with pests in the crops, Bruce noted that starlings ate the grass grubs, so instead of spraying the grubs he made over 140 small birdhouses for starlings to nest in. They were placed on a fence in each paddock. The starlings nested in the birdhouses and also ate the grubs.

The cattle yards, too, contain a lot of history. The steel for them came from the historic railway between Timaru and Fairlie: Bruce just happened to be at the sale. The old telephone poles between Tasman Downs and Tekapo have been put to good use in the yards as well. And when harvesting oats, Ian uses Bruce's old flying goggles to help protect his eyes from the dust.

Ian has made folding outdoor tables and chairs, lamps, tools, artwork and named each paddock using his metalwork skills by fashioning handmade signs from old hay rake tines. There are over 100 on the property, including *Linda's, Old Schoolhouse, The Nut that Changed My Life, Tussock Paddock, Chaff-cutter, Rabbiters, Jane's, Lilian's, Bruce's* and *Jack's*. Many gates have their own unique metalwork design. All have their own story. Perhaps most poignant is the metalwork Ian did for Bruce's grave, which sits high on a hill, just above where the old schoolhouse used to be all those years ago. It enjoys a very fine view.

The sheds at Tasman Downs are immaculate. The tools all have their place, and the floors are swept clean. A string in the workshop extends from one part of the rafters to another, supporting not Christmas cards but funeral service sheets. It is not at all morbid. Rather it is a moving tribute to loved high country people, some young, some old, who have died, but who are still remembered.

Bruce can rest easy. He proved the bureaucrats wrong and ensured that Tasman Downs remained an economic property in fine heart. As he put it at the end of his book, 'Life was never meant to be easy and challenges are put before us to be tackled, solved, avoided or accepted and made the best of. New Zealand is a wonderful country to live in.'[10]

ABOVE Ian Hayman dressed for the Tekapo Sales. MARY HOBBS
OPPOSITE The workshop at Tasman Downs. MARY HOBBS

THE WOLDS

On a clear, crisp day in the Mackenzie Country, the air is sharp and fresh. The autumn sun bathes the skin in warmth, until, all too soon, it slips behind the mountains and the temperature plunges. On any day such as this on The Wolds Station in the 1870s, the lone figure of the owner, William Saunders, may well have been glimpsed skating on the ice rink he had created beneath the willows. Apparently William was so adept that he could carve his name on the ice with his skates.[1] The rink has since fallen into disuse, but it is easy to imagine his graceful circumnavigation, watched over by the lofty, snow-capped peaks of the Main Divide in the distance. He put his talent to great use in the South Island high country, as there were social occasions in winter on various stations, such as Haldon and Irishman Creek, that inevitably seemed to include ice-skating or ice-hockey competitions.

William Saunders was the son of a successful hoop merchant in London, who had received a good education and 'as a traveller in manchester went as far afield as Russia', where he became an expert skater.[2] He arrived in New Zealand in 1855, via Victoria and New South Wales, and helped to explore and survey the Eyre and West Wakatipu area. He also assisted with the survey of the city of Dunedin and in the process met his lifelong friend, Alexander Smith. Left £40,000 when his father died in 1856, William took up Waipori Station in Otago, south-west of Dunedin and other freehold land in East Taieri.[3]

The mailbox at The Wolds. MARY HOBBS

Thomas Williamson Hall purchased The Wolds (excluding The Mary Range, which is now part of the station) between 1858 and 1859. William Ostler, later of Ben Ohau Station, managed it on his behalf. Both owner and manager were from Yorkshire, and they felt this landscape looked remarkably like the Yorkshire Wolds, a great treeless area of old glacial moraine, beneath huge open skies. William Saunders, then living at the Mistake, and Alexander Smith purchased the station in 1868. Alexander subsequently took over Rollesby Station and then sold his interest in The Wolds to his partner, who later bought The Mary Range and amalgamated it into The Wolds. This extended the property to the shores of Lake Pukaki.[4]

At the age of 48, William married Sarah Jane Luke (née Blake), the widow of an Oamaru chemist. After their marriage in 1875, William took his wife and stepson Willie to The Wolds, where they settled in a small cottage near the Maryburn River. He sold the Mistake in the same year.

They had barely settled into their home when Sarah became pregnant. She was at least a full day's travel on horseback from the company of another woman. The journey was rough, as there were only faint tracks, if anything, across this immense country of tussock, spaniard and matagouri. In that first year she could be found among the tussocks planting primroses and violets[5] along a path, in a valiant attempt to make a garden in the glacial, silt-like earth, just like other pioneer women around New Zealand.

Sarah gave birth to her second son, John, in Timaru in July 1876 but only months later, on 13 September, nine-year-old Willie died of convulsions that lasted between two and 20 hours. He is buried in the Burkes Pass Cemetery. Then, just nine days later, Sarah also died, aged only 30. The cause listed on the death certificate is difficult to decipher, but it appears she suffered from pyaemia (a type of septicaemia) for six weeks and exhaustion for four weeks. It is probable that Sarah initially contracted the infection during childbirth. She is buried in Timaru. Her infant son, John, was cared for by other Mackenzie women, particularly Catherine Burnett of Mount Cook Station. In the summer of that year of tragedy, five-month-old John died of bronchitis on 28 December 1876. Within four months William had lost his stepson, his wife and his son.

A seat in the garden at The Wolds. MARY HOBBS

William continued to live at The Wolds. A married couple, Mr and Mrs McDonald, and their sons, managed the station and lived in the house that is now the homestead, to the south of the Saunders' cottage. The garden Sarah had tenderly planted between the tussocks, on either side of the path between the two homes, became forbidden territory. The grief-stricken William would allow no one to walk there.

He lived at The Wolds for another three decades, though he increasingly kept to the seclusion of his library and gradually became more of a recluse. He eventually sold the station and retired to Timaru, where he lived in the Grosvenor Hotel. He died on 4 September 1917 at 90 years of age. An obituary in the *Timaru Herald* described him as 'a considerate neighbour, a liberal and even generous employer, and highly respected resident'. Although 'of a very retiring disposition' he always assisted the advancement of both the Mackenzie Country and New Zealand whenever he could, 'and no appeal for help was made in vain'.[6]

William Grant bought The Wolds, including Irishman Creek, from William Saunders in 1902. Like many a high country station owner, William and his older brother Andrew came from Scotland, in this case Ross-shire. When they arrived in New Zealand early in 1865, Charles Tripp of Orari Gorge Station, who was in search of a good shepherd, spotted the Grants' excellent sheepdog as the men left the ship at Timaru and hired both brothers on the spot. Andrew later became manager of Orari Gorge.

At one time or another William, who became a successful stock dealer, owned a variety of stations in the Mackenzie Country, but his main home and place of residence was Elloughton Grange Farm just outside Timaru, so although he owned The Wolds, he did not live there. In the 1880s, when the frozen meat trade began, William took advantage of the new opportunity, handling consignments for the owners and becoming a very wealthy man. Later in life, he concentrated on his land and financial interests, 'investing most of his fortune in first mortgages, usually to Scots, and often with a genuine helpfulness'.[7] According to William Vance, both brothers 'were regarded as good employers and helped their men on to properties of their own'.[8] Once, when William observed a station owner abandoning his station and making his way down the road, he told him to return to the station, as he would back him. The man did so

Murrays have owned Rhoborough, Braemar, Sawdon, Glenmore, Godley Peaks and Glentanner stations. Today, different branches of the Murray family continue to run Glenmore, Maryburn and The Wolds.

After Braemar was sold, Tim Murray (Michael's brother) was keen to procure Maryburn Station, next to The Wolds on State Highway 8, but was worried he would not get it. He asked Michael to put a bid in for The Wolds, so that at least he would have one of the two stations. Michael and Caro had been considering a move to North Canterbury, but Michael put the bid in for his brother anyway. Tim ended up with Maryburn, the station he had preferred, and Michael's bid was also accepted, so he and Caro moved to The Wolds.

It was a wrench to leave Braemar, as both Michael and Caro adored their home, with its sublime views up towards Aoraki/Mt Cook. When they arrived at The Wolds, with their two young children, John and Sue, they were greatly disappointed to find the station and the house in an advanced state of disrepair. The head of an old iron bed, attached to the fence around the house by two old dog collars, was doing service as the front gate. The original cottage where William and Sarah Saunders had lived was uninhabitable. The walls were made of totara boards and gravel was used as a form of insulation between the outer and inner walls. When the totara moved, which it did, the stones fell out, leaving little in the way of structure. It was still decorated with exquisite William Morris-style wallpapers, almost certainly selected by William and Sarah a century before. There were two front rooms and two back rooms, with a stone fireplace in each and a hallway down the middle. The outside chimneys were gargantuan and seemed out of proportion to the little cottage. Caro and Michael's children put the old place to use by doing their Correspondence School work there.

The family who had lived in the house behind and to the south of the Saunders' cottage managed the station on behalf of the Grant family for many years. They had six children. Caro was in awe of the wife, wondering how she coped in such conditions with so many children. It seemed that the previous owner had not invested in the upkeep of the houses and visited infrequently, if at all. There was also a difference of opinion on the definition of supplies, as when the manager asked the owner for more supplies, several cases of whisky would turn up, but little else!

The easterly wind was bitingly cold. It swooped around the exposed

and several years later became a successful runholder. In 1910, aged 65, William died from an aneurysm of the heart. His obituary in the *Timaru Herald* described him as 'quiet and unassuming, always treating everyone alike'.[9] The Grant family owned The Wolds for 55 years, at which point it was subdivided into three blocks.

In 1957 Michael Murray, son of Bruce and Lu, purchased the 7000-hectare homestead block, which included the old cottage where William and Sarah Saunders had lived.

The Murrays have a long association with the Mackenzie. Michael Murray's grandfather, George Murray, purchased Sawdon Station and a series of others before settling at Braemar. Over the generations, the

ABOVE The old Saunders' cottage after a winter snowfall. MURRAY FAMILY COLLECTION
OPPOSITE Caro Murray holds the horses in front of a hut on the Mary Range, while out mustering. MURRAY FAMILY COLLECTION

side of the house, making it even more miserable. The drain from the bath ran out onto the ground. There was no flush toilet but there were two long drops built back to back. The laundry was down by the creek with a copper. The pipes supplying water to the house lay on top of the ground, and froze in winter. There was no power when they first moved in, only a ghastly diesel generator for lighting that rattled and hissed and was difficult to get started. The house was made of corrugated iron with no insulation. In winter it was so cold that a glass of water left overnight would freeze; temperatures often reached -13°C. Ferrets also found their way into the house. The first thing Michael did was remove the iron cladding and replace it with wood. A septic tank was put in and the plumbing was attended to. Things slowly improved.

Not long after they moved, Evelyn Hosken of Simons Hill, who many described in those days as the Matriarch of the Mackenzie, arrived with a huge jar of jam she had made. It was a year or two old, but Evelyn showed Caro how to carefully scrape the top off and boil the jam again to make it fresh. Things had to last. Nothing was wasted. Food was purchased in bulk, as trips into town were rare, though the Murrays had an old car they pressed into service when required.

In the 1950s a car could only be purchased with overseas funds. Caro's grandmother had left her some overseas shares, so they eventually traded their old car in and purchased a Holden, but new tyres were hard to obtain, so journeys were planned carefully in order to make the tyres last.

squeezed in, too, with visitors regularly arriving at the station, often en route to other places. There were family picnics, a spot of fishing every now and then, and church on some Sundays.

There were many challenges, including the demands made by some shearers, who required a flush toilet in the woolshed before they would work, despite there being flush toilets in the cookhouse and in their quarters. Michael and Caro had electricity, water and the septic tank put out there, and finally, the toilet. Peace reigned. But one day Caro was near the cookhouse looking for eggs when she looked up to see all the shearers standing outside the men's quarters peeing off the verandah.

Cooking dinners for contractors could also be a challenging experience. One day Caro daringly served curried sausages, only to be asked, 'What's this muck you're trying to feed us?' Undaunted, she tried them on pizza. That did not go down too well either. When the contractors' cook arrived she made scones with pumpkin added. No, they would have none of that. The cook sent it back with a meringue on top for afternoon tea and they ate it without noticing. For the main meals, though, Caro returned to the tried and true meat and spuds.

Michael and Caro had taken on a tremendous responsibility, not only with all the station work and immediate repair, but also because Michael was elected as both county chairman and as local chairman of Federated Farmers. This carried on a tradition, as the Murray family had served on the council for three generations. Caro supported Michael in his public roles and both were also actively involved with the Church of the Good Shepherd. Despite the challenges, it was a fulfilling and busy life. The Mackenzie was, very definitely, home.

Outside influences were the source of their main challenges and the biggest of these was the hydro scheme. There was no advance warning that the dams and canals were planned when Michael and Caro purchased the station. Michael advocated, in an unpaid capacity, on behalf of runholders who had major concerns about the raising of the lakes and the corresponding loss of farmland around Lakes Tekapo, Pukaki and the new Lake Benmore. All stations surrounding these lakes lost some of their most productive and fertile farmland, which made several stations almost unviable. For The Wolds, the most devastating blow was the loss of their land on the banks of Lake Pukaki, as well as all their land on the north side

Fencing on the property was almost non-existent, with only two boundary fences and two paddocks fenced off, one for rams and one for sheep, so a great deal had to be done to make the station viable. Michael spent weeks in the cold and rain erecting new fences.

Like most runholders, Michael kept a farm diary. The entries are concise, yet they faithfully tell the story of the daily tasks on a high country station in that era. His days were filled with mustering, sheep dipping, crutching, shearing, selling stock, buying stock, putting rams to sheep, lambing, rabbit poisoning meetings, grading drives, killing mutton, helping neighbours, fencing and mending equipment. Family life was

ABOVE Caro and the children watch the hydro earthworks. MURRAY FAMILY COLLECTION
OPPOSITE Excerpts from Michael Murray's farm diary. MARY HOBBS

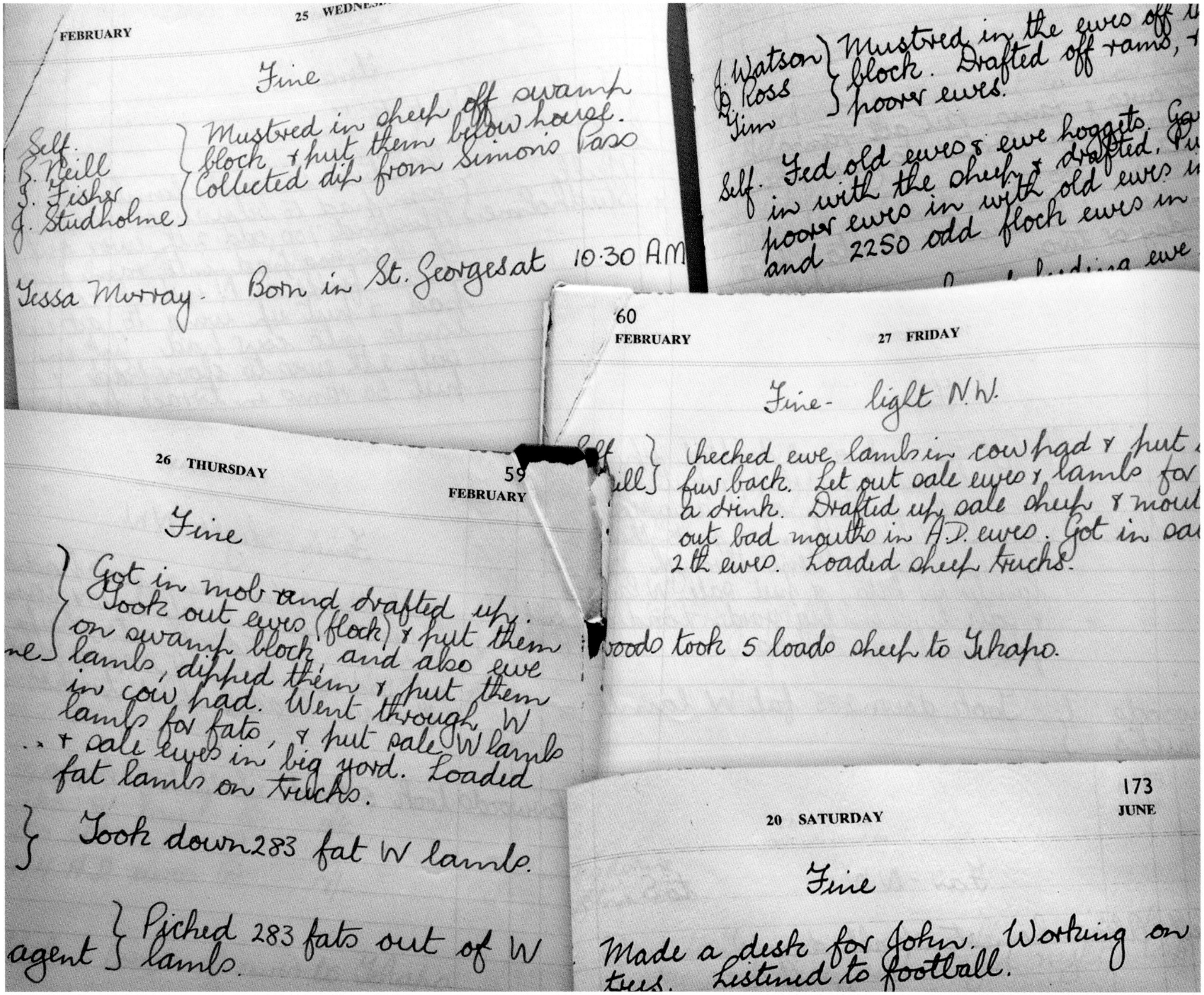

25 WEDNESDAY

Fine

Self
J. Neill
J. Fisher
J. Studholme }
Mustered in sheep off swamp block & put them below house. Collected dip from Simons Pass

Tessa Murray. Born in St. Georges at 10.30 A.M.

---

26 THURSDAY

59
FEBRUARY

Fine

} Got in mob and drafted up. Took out ewes (flock) & put them on swamp block, and also ewe lambs, dipped them & put them in cow pad. Went through W lambs for fats, & put sale W lambs + sale ewes in big yard. Loaded fat lambs on trucks.

} Took down 283 fat W lambs.

agent } Picked 283 fats out of W lambs.

J. Watson
J. Ross
Tim }
Mustered in the ewes off block. Drafted off rams, poorer ewes.

Self. Fed old ewes & ewe hoggets in with the sheep. Drafted poorer ewes in with old ewes and 2250 odd flock ewes in
... including ewe

60
FEBRUARY

27 FRIDAY

Fine - light N.W.

Self }
ll }
checked ewe lambs in cowpad & put few back. Let out sale ewes & lambs for a drink. Drafted up sale sheep & moul... out bad mouths in A.P. ewes. Got in sale 2 th ewes. Loaded sheep trucks.

...woods took 5 loads sheep to Tekapo.

173
JUNE

20 SATURDAY

Fine

.. Made a desk for John. Working on trees. Listened to football.

of the canal and beside the Tekapo River, which removed direct access to the river and lake. They were offered some free troughs for their stock to get water in the future – a woefully inadequate substitute.

The building of canals by the Ministry of Works (MOW) caused great upheaval. One day the ministry arrived at The Wolds with bulldozers and, without bothering to go through the gate, just ploughed on through the fence. Within minutes Michael was on the phone to the Minister of Lands and the bulldozers were, at least on that particular day, ordered to retreat. On other occasions the MOW left deep ruts over the land, with holes dug at varying intervals to see if there was sand beneath that could be used for the canals. The holes, over 6 metres deep, were left open, which made the area dangerous for stock.

The other problem was dust, tonnes of it, spread over the property, and dusty wool fetches far less on the market than clean wool. It took years for the damage to be remediated and little compensation was provided for the devalued wool clip. Meanwhile, the water in local rivers became black and almost unusable. Michael suggested the MOW divert water to the house from a spring further up, but the advice was ignored. Finally they had to go back to what Michael suggested in the first place.

The farmers asked, sensibly, for future irrigation outlets to be incorporated into the works but this was refused and now, years later, everyone has to siphon water out. Sheep occasionally went missing, taken by the workers without asking, and little warning was given of work being done. One day Michael and Caro, unaware of any blasting in a particular area of the station, came around a corner on their way home from mustering to be greeted by a huge explosion.

At one point the government proposed flooding one of the old swamps on the station, but this would have made The Wolds uneconomic, so for 10 years the Murray family lived under the constant threat of losing their station and postponed upkeep and building plans, until the idea was finally rejected. However the gain from all the pain was that irrigation became available to The Wolds, which made all the difference to its viability.

The Murrays were also caught out when they extended second mortgages to station holders and other businesses to help them get started because, at one particular point, the incumbent government cancelled all second mortgages. With the stroke of a pen, the family lost a substantial amount of their personal savings. A number of those businesses and stations went on to thrive, but the Murrays, and others in similar situations, were never compensated.

The great stress resulting from all these challenges made Michael very ill, initially with mumps. He was also rammed by a sheep in the yard, which caused acute back pain that developed into a lingering ailment. Months later, it was discovered that he had cracked his pelvis. Despite an operation, the problems with Michael's back were never resolved.

Caro and Michael had been planning a trip overseas, but as the time to depart came closer it was apparent Michael was not fit enough. He urged Caro to go, promising he would join her as soon as possible. She

set off reluctantly, but was also excited about her great adventure. She had been gone for a week, and was in Switzerland when she received a call from a friend, a doctor in New Zealand, urging her to take the next flight home. In shock, and still wearing her trekking boots, she took a taxi to Rome to connect with a flight home. Then the plane broke down in Singapore.

Although Michael had been ill, no one had suspected that there was another underlying serious illness. After Caro's return, Michael lived a few more months and then died in 1977, at the age of 49. He left the farm to his son John, who immediately came home from Lincoln College, where he had recently graduated with a BSc. He married Bronwen McKenzie the following November and then took over the station. Caro felt adrift.

She and Michael had a section in Tekapo where they had intended to build their retirement home, so Caro began the building and later did the painting. She put her love of skiing to good use by becoming a ski patroller at Round Hill for two seasons. Encouraged by Audrey Burtscher of Richmond Station, she went back to Europe to finish her trip and worked there for several years. When Caro returned to New Zealand she was a Mackenzie District councillor for six years, but became frustrated with the rules that seemed to block positive changes. Self-sufficient and determined, she now lives in Christchurch.

John Murray had to take on a large mortgage, manage the station and put sufficient money into keeping it viable, all while dealing with the grief of losing his father prematurely. The first major hurdle was finding the money to pay death duties, the third time the Murray family had to do so on the same assets. This crippling tax was abolished in 1992.

Bronwen, the daughter of a well-known Timaru surgeon, describes life as a young bride in the middle of the Mackenzie Country as a baptism beyond fire. She could not cook when she first arrived, and so a great deal in the way of rice risotto was served. Nor did the men let her forget the time she served carrots slightly warm, rather than cooked. As well as

culinary challenges, the house was falling down about their ears. In the first year on the station she also became pregnant with her first son, Huw. But, like her stoic pioneering predecessors, Bronwen just had to 'get on with it'. She enrolled in some cooking classes and became a first-rate cook. With that under her belt, she turned her attention to her young family – she had a second son, Bryn – and helped out at the Tekapo playcentre. The remoteness of The Wolds meant that the boys both went to boarding school, which was a great wrench for Bronwen. Huw is now regional manager for Agriseeds, and lives near Dunedin with his wife, Anna, and their two daughters, Eloise and Georgia. Bryn, after graduating with a BCom, returned to work on the station, and lives at The Wolds with his wife Kimberley and their two daughters, Indya and Arabella.

Other station holders speak of the Murrays with respect. They are known as kind, good-hearted, generous people. John's skill in farming and his astuteness when serving on Federated Farmers has not gone unnoticed, as he has contributed a great deal towards getting farmers to work together.

The next time you buy an Icebreaker merino garment, take a look at the code on the label: the origin of the wool may well be The Wolds Station. In a brief video on the Icebreaker website, John speaks of his love for this land and the station, and what he produces. He is passionate about the future of wool and its obvious advantages over synthetic products.

The environment here is a challenge but we love it. In winter we feed out silage to the sheep – it takes six hours a day. When it snows, feeding-out is virtually a full-time job for three people. The longest the snow has hung around is about eight weeks; the only food the stock can get is what you feed them. We've got to keep them in good condition so that they grow good fibre …

In a rare moment, John reflects on the beauty of this place he calls home. He describes a land that is immense, where the light changes as it reflects on the hills and where the view is different every day.

OPPOSITE Early dawn over The Mary Range, now part of The Wolds. MARY HOBBS

GLENTANNER

Ed Dark was a man on a mission. He and his brother Cornelius emigrated from England in 1856, started up a business making cob cottages in Nelson, travelled further south and took possession of Glentanner Station in 1858, and then stocked it with sheep that took Ed 18 months to drove from Nelson to the Mackenzie.

This left little in the way of time for the domestic side of life, which is possibly why the Dark brothers remained bachelors. One day, when Ed needed a clean shirt for a cattle sale in Timaru, he looked at his scant wardrobe and found he was completely out – not that he probably had more than two or three. This did not worry him for long. Down to the creek he went, where he gave his shirt a good dousing, and then, after tying the sleeves around his shoulders, he was off at a gallop with his shirt billowing gaily in the wind behind him. It was probably dry before he got to Pukaki.

Ed's first home in the Mackenzie was more like a bivvy, as for several years he bunked down under an overhanging rock near the lake.[1] He later built a homestead near Boundary Stream, close to what was then the head of Lake Pukaki. Ed named his property Glentanner, apparently after the ship that brought him and his brother to New Zealand.

In the words of T.D. Burnett, like Big Mick of Birch Hill, Ed, known as Old Dark, 'hated globe-trotting tourists with a great and healthy hatred'. He had no time for 'Londoners of wealth … [who] thought the back

---

The home paddocks at Glentanner Station. MARY HOBBS

gorge stations were simply there to put them up … the wealthy cockney thought he was doing everything necessary if he talked "shop," praised the scones and butter'. On one occasion, several visitors 'were put up for the night and strove hard to be agreeable, but their thoughts and expressions underwent a great change when Dark put them to bunk in an out hut infested with fleas'. The next morning he was 'seen speeding his disappearing guests by waving his arms, "Goodbye, my love, Good-bye"'. For other visitors, especially South Islanders, he could not do enough.[2]

Old Dark had some good men working with him and John Brown, from the Isle of Skye, was one, known to be a steady and reliable influence. One day he was out snow-raking for sheep with a mate called Browning. They were working slightly different areas: John was further up Freds Stream, almost 10 kilometres from Glentanner homestead. Browning returned to camp and, as John was not there, assumed he must have returned to the homestead. About three days later, when Browning arrived back at the homestead, there was no sign of his mate. A search began immediately, the men looking for a mustering stick standing in the snow, the sign left by Highland shepherds.

It was Big Mick who found the mustering stick with John's hat hanging on top. His body was found in a snowdrift beneath it. John Brown was placed in a coffin of native birch made by a station hand and lined with a grey blanket. He was buried on Birch Hill Station.[3] The inscription on the headstone is opposite.

Despite some ups and downs, and the odd skirmish with neighbours, and each other, Old Dark and Cornelius seemed happy at Glentanner and lived there for about 20 years. Cornelius died in late 1881 or early in 1882, aged about 54. His brother Ed found it hard to keep going alone, so sold the station in 1884 to the Thomson brothers, Robert and George. Robert subsequently lived on the station with their sister.

On 7 December 1885 Miss Thomson was playing the piano in the parlour at the front of the homestead, which had a clear view of the lake. As she played, she glimpsed the station whaleboat drifting by, empty.[4] George, who was visiting the station, had gone across the lake to collect the mail. As the newspapers reported, since 'there was no wind to upset the boat, it is supposed he jumped out when near the shore, and sank in a quicksand. His hat and the boat were found floating near the shore.' His body was never recovered. After the tragedy, Robert and his sister lost all heart for Glentanner. They sold up in 1887 and moved back to England.

A man named James Brown then owned the station for about five years, after which it passed to Alexander Herdman and then back to Brown again. Brown was unfortunate enough to face the bad snow of 1888, when the woolshed blew away, and then the terrible snowfall of 1895.

Mountain guide Jack Adamson, who was working at the Hermitage that year, recalled that a man called Gibson was helping the Glentanner manager, John Ross, bring sheep from the high ground down to the flats when Gibson became frozen to the saddle and had to tear himself off it. He walked to the house with his body bent in the same posture as when he was riding the horse: his trousers were frozen solid. Water left in the kettles on the stove at Glentanner froze overnight, and fowls froze to death on their perches. Those at Birch Hill Station were snowed in for about 10 weeks. A record 2.3 metres of snow fell.[5]

Brown found it difficult to recover from losing 2000 head of stock, and so the station was put up for sale. In August 1896 he sold 'the goodwill of the lease, the freehold, the plant, 6,000 merinos, 80 cattle, and 20 horses' to Bernard and Jack Tripp and Simon McKenzie for just £1200.[6]

SACRED

to the memory

OF

JOHN BROWN
AN ISLE OF SKYE MAN WHO WAS
LOST NEAR THIS SPOT IN THE SNOW
OF 1870
AGED 32
A KIND NEIGHBOUR, A FIRST CLASS
SHEEPMAN, AND ONE NOTED FOR HIS
GOOD DOGS.
Among pastures green he'll lead his flock,
where living streams appear;
And GOD the LORD from ev'ry eye,
shall wipe off ev'ry tear.

———— ————

THOSE WHO COME AFTER ARE ASKED TO
TAKE CARE OF THIS GRAVE AND OF
JIMMY LLOYD'S, BIRCH HILL.

FRIENDS 1901.

Jack, who managed Glentanner, enjoyed the station, which in those days extended from Birch Hill Station to Boundary Stream, so it included what is now known as Ferintosh Station. He particularly loved the outlook, with tall peaks in almost every direction, as far as the eye could see.

A mail coach came to the Hermitage once a week in summer, though sometimes it was caught out in bad weather and the drivers and passengers would then troop into Glentanner for shelter. On one occasion Jack Tripp remembered that 22 people stayed overnight, with some even

ABOVE John Brown's headstone. MARY HOBBS
OPPOSITE The Big Snow of 1895. JACK ADAMSON COLLECTION

sleeping under the carpet to keep warm. The boys at Glentanner had six towels between them, which they gallantly handed out to the women in the group. When the visitors left, Glentanner's stock of jam had all been eaten and there was no more due until the next supply came through.

The weather was always variable. Sudden storms could catch travellers out, with little warning. In 1895, Mr Weir, a travelling salesman from Oamaru, almost drowned on his way to the Hermitage.[7] It is unclear what he was doing so far from Oamaru, but there he was, optimistically leaving Glentanner Station on the morning of 17 December, bound for the Hermitage. He came across John Ross, so they convivially made their way up to the hotel together, just as a huge thunderstorm struck. They made a frantic dash back to Glentanner, but had not anticipated the rapid rise of the rivers. By some miracle, they finally made it to Birch Hill. So far, so good.

Unwisely, they pressed on. Both driving buggies, they crossed Tin Hut Creek, now known as Freds Stream, without mishap. However, when they arrived at Bush Stream they found the deluge had turned it into a river of violently rolling boulders coursing down the riverbed. It seemed impossible to cross, so they made their way back to Birch Hill Station. Unfortunately, by this time Tin Hut Creek had risen dramatically. Once again optimism and a careless regard for the conditions reigned, so Mr Weir entered the river. What could possibly go wrong?

Immediately the buggy capsized, his horse disappeared and he was tossed into the maelstrom, finally making it to a small spit in the river. The horse and buggy were found further down. Sadly, his horse had drowned. Mr Weir then struck out from the spit for the nearest land. Again he was carried downstream but finally got over to the Birch Hill side and hurried off to get assistance. By the time he arrived back at the boundary creek between Glentanner and Birch Hill, it was also going at a 'terrific rate'.[8] When he tried to cross, he received a severe drubbing and was carried another kilometre or more downstream, until the creek finally dumped him on the same side he went in on. He hobbled back to John Ross. They waited until noon for the creek levels to subside and finally reached Glentanner at 4 p.m.

Jack Tripp was well aware of the land's other hidden dangers. He recalled three people had died in the quicksands near Lake Pukaki,

including a man with his horse and buggy. When they searched for him, a hat was all that remained. For these reasons, Jack had a healthy wariness about crossing the Tasman River. He remembered several floods so great that the Tasman flowed from bank to bank, and one summer he crossed 42 streams, some of them 100 metres wide.

Leopold George Dyke Acland was the next owner of Glentanner. He purchased the station in 1897, and had gained experience in high country sheepfarming since leaving school in 1893. He left the station in February 1900, to serve in the 3rd Contingent of the Rough Riders who went to the South African War with their own horses. He returned in March of 1901.

In 1904, Leo travelled from Fairlie to Glentanner with George Murray and his guest, Captain Scott, who had just returned from Antarctica, but had made a detour to visit Mount Cook and the glaciers before his ship, the *Discovery*, sailed from Lyttelton.

Leo, who was very interested in history, wrote a number of articles for the *Press*, as well as *The Early Canterbury Runs*, published in 1930, in which he mentioned the good men who worked for him at Glentanner, particularly overseer John Carmichael, who was later a partner at Birch Hill Station: 'He was one of the best shepherds that ever came to the country and could walk through Merino sheep on a hillside and disturb them as little as most men would disturb crossbreds.'

John was also very superstitious. When Leo told him one year that an unusual number of deformed lambs had been born at Mount Peel, he replied, 'Oh, that's no' a good sign, there's no luck in the like o' that.' Leo was 'glad to be able to confirm his opinion by telling him that the '95 winter which very nearly ruined …the owner, had followed that lambing'. The following spring, there were far more black lambs than usual at Glentanner. 'I asked John whether this also portended bad luck. "No, no, black lambs is the sign of an increasing business," said John. Sure enough, I had one of the best years I ever had.'[9] Three years later, Leo sold Glentanner to George Murray.

Leo then purchased and sold another station in Amuri, and went on a tour to India. While there he shot and wounded a tiger, which then turned and lunged for him. Leo stood his ground and fired again, but the tiger dragged him off into the bush. Luckily, a local man then dispatched the animal. After an 18-hour trip to hospital, Leo lost his left arm. His right arm was also injured, but this did not slow him down. Before long he was off to Japan, where he managed a shipping office, then he travelled to Moscow and St Petersburg on the Trans-Siberian Railway. He returned to England, and then New Zealand, where he bought and sold several other stations.

Despite being 38, and having only one arm, he fought in the First World War, as a second lieutenant with the Army Service Corps, winning the Military Cross at Gallipoli. He was promoted to major and also awarded an OBE for 'valuable service in connection with the war'.[10]

At the time of his death in Sumner, Christchurch, in 1948, Leo owned Cecil Peak Station on Lake Wakatipu. He was 'an expert conversationalist, and famed for his fund of stories, not all of them printable, of early days in Canterbury'.[11] A tarn north of Freds Stream and south of Glentanner Station, near a monument acknowledging the early pioneers who built the Mount Cook Road, is called Acland Lagoon. It seems fitting that something in this wild landscape bears his name.

George Murray sold Glentanner Station in 1913 to Edwin Rowland Guinness, a well-liked man whose ancestors were related to the founders of the famous Irish drink. Edwin's father, Frank Guinness, was a cousin of Michael Burke, who had written extolling the great virtues of life in New Zealand. Frank embarked with his family to check it out and settled here.

After a successful stint at auctioneering, Edwin formed a stock and station firm with Henry Le Cren. Guinness and Le Cren was later

LEFT Leo Acland and his wife enjoying their honeymoon in Europe. MR AND MRS J. ACLAND FAMILY COLLECTION
OPPOSITE Mustering sheep along the Mount Cook Road toward Glentanner Station, 1950s. SOUTH CANTERBURY MUSEUM

amalgamated with Pyne and Gould and the company became known as Pyne, Gould, Guinness. Edwin and Henry enjoyed a close association in the high country, as Henry had purchased Birch Hill Station in the same year that Edwin purchased Glentanner.

Edwin had the habit of taking his son Rowland with him when he visited the high country and Rowland was particularly fond of Glentanner, especially when Alex Robertson and his wife were managing it. Mrs Robertson awakened in Rowland a lifelong interest in native plants. William Vance describes one occasion when the Robertsons, Henry Le Cren, Edwin Guinness and others enjoyed a picnic at the Blue Lake, near the Tasman Glacier, where Mrs Robertson showed them different native flowers in bloom. The picnic became an enjoyable annual event.[12]

For Mrs Robertson, the native plants were possibly a reminder of her beloved brother, mountain guide Jock Richmond, who had introduced her to the native gentians, edelweiss, Mount Cook lilies and mountain daisies that grew in the area. Jock had been guiding at Mount Cook for three years when, in February 1914, he and fellow guide Darby Thompson accompanied a client, experienced climber Sydney King, up the mountain. They were caught by a devastating avalanche that cascaded from the formidable ice cliffs overhanging the Linda Glacier. The three men were killed instantly. Jock's body was the only one found.

Jock's fiancée was waiting for him at the old Hermitage, and his sister was at Glentanner. It was a sad year for the guiding community and the district. Both guides were well liked and highly respected. One newspaper account reported that Darby Thompson ' strangely enough, seems to have had some premonition of disaster'. In a discussion about the perils of mountaineering with a Christchurch resident, he 'referred to the fact that there had been no fatal accidents among the guides in the Mount Cook district. "All the same," he said, "we carry our lives in our hands. Don't be surprised if you hear soon that one of us has met his Waterloo.""[13]

The Robertsons managed Glentanner Station for 25 years, after which their son took over. Keith Stirling then became manager. A postcard of Keith, his horse and a flock of sheep, with Aoraki/Mt Cook in the background, is probably one of the best-known images in New Zealand. Keith managed the station until 1957, when Ian Ivey came to manage the property, after having purchased a share in it.

Eventually Ian and his wife Pat purchased the station outright. Ian built an excellent new woolshed, which is still in use today. After a protracted battle with the local council, Ian expanded activities on the station in 1975 to include tourism, which has proved very successful.

The ownership of the station passed from Ian to his son Ross and wife Helen, who have run it for many years, with the main stock including merino sheep, Hereford cattle and red deer. Ross and Helen's eldest son, Mark, and his wife Kate, have three children and live on the station. Mark increasingly manages the property, and Ross is still involved, although possibly less so since becoming a grower director on the Board of New Zealand Merino. Helen oversees the tourism ventures at Glentanner. Ross and Helen also have a daughter, Sarah, and another son, George. The station is carefully nurtured by the Iveys and is in fine form. Glentanner was recently freeholded under tenure review and much of the land has been retired back to the Crown, with the rest remaining under the ownership of the Ivey family.

There are many streams on the way to Glentanner Station and on the main road to Aoraki/Mount Cook, most named after shepherds who worked at the station in the early years. Jacks Creek and Freds Stream recall Jack Kay and Fred Baker, who were both shepherds at Glentanner in the 1860s.[14] Whale Stream was apparently named in memory of the old whaleboat used by Glentanner. Birch Hill Stream marked the old boundary between Glentanner and Birch Hill Station. As the sign there still says, when you cross the bridge over this stream you're 'above the worry line'. Bush Stream is the river flowing out of a bush-covered valley from which timber was taken to build homesteads, and also ferried across to Mount Cook Station for building material. It was a long way to go to get firewood.

Twin Stream (or The Twins Stream, depending on who you talk to) is named after two streams flowing closely together. They were prone to frequent flooding in the old days and caused havoc for coach drivers en route to the Hermitage, who would often enquire of travellers coming from Mount Cook, 'How are the twins today?' – to the mystification of

their passengers. If Twin Stream was high, the drivers would ferry their charges across. Twin Stream was also where Jack Adamson's wife, Nora, crossed the flooded river with her new baby (see p. 35).

Boundary Stream was originally the boundary between Rhoborough Downs and Glentanner. Later subdivision of the high country changed this, and it is now the boundary between Ferintosh and Pukaki Downs. In the 1800s, Glentanner homestead was in the vicinity of Boundary Stream, where Lake Pukaki originally ended. With the first raising of the lake, it extended to Jacks Stream. With the second, and final raising of the lake, it extended to the Glentanner airstrip.

Another homestead, located on the site of the current main house, was burnt down when lightning struck its telephone wires in a storm on Christmas Day of 1949. A new house was built soon after and sits on the same spot.

The Rest is an area situated between the old Hermitage and Pukaki, on the edge of the lake. Remains of the old track to this area can still be seen. This beautiful spot was where coaches stopped, passengers had a meal and horses were swapped over. There was just a caretaker's cottage, stables and a shed there in the 1800s. Later, Ministry of Works buildings were built in the same area. Now it is barren, except for the remains of some foundations, which may be glimpsed when the lake is calm and low. It remains a great place for a traveller to stop, sit a while and take in the spectacular scenery.

Merinos wait to be shorn at Glentanner. MARY HOBBS

FERINTOSH

In the 1950s, Gilbert Seymour was probably the first person to climb Aoraki/Mt Cook, guided by the legendary mountain guide, Harry Ayres, and then fly a plane solo over the summit just over a month later.

New Zealand's highest mountain is a serious climb, not particularly for its pitch, but more because of the hazards. Ice cliffs hang over the route at awkward intervals, and climbers have no real control over when avalanches may cascade down from formidably high ice towers, which are often on a terrifying lean. There is nowhere to go to escape the danger, so, carefully placing one foot after the other, climbers have to read the weather properly and hope fervently that they will be safe as they move up the route beneath.

Gilbert has always been known as a steady, calm influence, so it is likely that these attributes served him well in his mountaineering days. He has mustered on many famous Canterbury and South Canterbury stations, including Mesopotamia, Mount Algidus, Mount Oakden, Hakatere, Black Forest, Simons Hill, Simons Pass, Mount Cook, Glentanner, Rhoborough, Pukaki Downs, Birch Hill and Braemar, to name just a few. High country farming is in his DNA.

Gilbert is now in his late eighties and in fine health. Blessed with excellent eyesight, hearing and a sharp, alert mind, he continues to tend

Late autumn sun highlights Ferintosh Station on the western shores of Lake Pukaki.
MARY HOBBS

112

end of the day, the billy was boiling and their cheerful talk could be heard on the step where Gilbert sat, looking out to the great country beyond. Dust motes danced in the last rays of the setting sun, which fought with the creeping cold to keep the worst of the chill off tired limbs and aching feet. Gilbert realised then that there was no other place he wanted to be. From that point on his destiny remained irrevocably entwined with Ferintosh, one of the most beautiful high country stations of them all.

Although christened Albert Raincliff Seymour, Gilbert's father was known simply as Bill. (The name Raincliff was after the station on which his father worked and where the family then lived.) He was born in 1880 to William Dionysius Seymour and Sarah Seymour (née Hobbs) and grew up in South Canterbury. Bill's father died in 1882 at the age of 31. Several years later, his mother Sarah remarried. Bill was just 16 when she died.

As a young lad, Bill began working as a teamster for one of the Grant brothers at Elloughton Grange near Timaru. William and Andrew Grant had bought and sold many stations in the Mackenzie, sometimes in partnership with each other and at other times individually. One day, Andrew Burnett of Mount Cook Station was in Timaru and asked the Grants if there was a 'likely lad' available to work for him. He was told he should probably take young Seymour, as 'his eyes are always peeled towards the hills'.

From that day on, Bill became a man of the Mackenzie. He began work for Andrew Burnett as a shepherd in approximately 1899 or 1900. Seven years later he became the manager of Mount Cook Station and, despite buying his own station during that time, remained in that role for a further 20 years, working for both Andrew and T.D. Burnett.

T.D. spoke very highly of Bill and regarded him as one of his most valued shepherds. He used to say that Bill could slide so far down a frozen slope and pick himself up again unharmed and unshaken that he was christened 'the champion snow-slider of the Mackenzie Country'.[1] He was also renowned throughout the Mackenzie for his skills at baking camp oven bread and was a crack shot with a rifle.

Bill was very much his own man and kept his own counsel. As William Vance noted, whether it was crossing rivers, mustering in snow or working on the Tasman Islands pocketed with quicksands, nothing held any fear for Bill. He was known to take very good care of his dogs, which, in those days was an excellent measure of the character of a man. Bill only

his home garden, which feeds him and his wife, Marion, well. He keeps fit by walking many kilometres as he goes about daily jobs on Ferintosh.

He clearly remembers the day, as a teenager in the 1940s, when he made a momentous decision about his future, while helping out with a muster. The men had all returned to one of the outlying huts towards the ever had three dogs with him and they were always in excellent condition. He could speak to them, though not necessarily always with words. He was also skilled with horses.

In 1915 Bill purchased a half-share of Lilybank Station at the head of Lake Tekapo with fellow shepherd, Rex Malthus. The natural boundaries of the station were the Godley and Macauley rivers, and the Main Divide. It is not country for the faint-hearted. Seymour Peak, at the head of the Godley, was named in honour of Bill's time there.

In *High Country Family*, Betty Dick mentions that when Rex and Bill took over Lilybank, they sold off the sheep on the station cheaply and brought in merinos. At that time, they also had trouble with kea and substantial snowfalls. However, they built huts, sheds, yards, sheep dips and worked hard to get fencing and other vital jobs done to make the station more viable.[2]

Jock Mackinnon, who had been on the station since 1904, had a good store of knowledge for Bill and Rex to draw on. Jock's wife was apparently an outstanding woman, who coped with the very primitive conditions in one of the most remote stations in the country. She always made sure all the men ate well and is remembered with great respect and fondness.

In February 1917 Bill was called up as part of the fourth conscription ballot, but he was stood down, as work on stations was regarded as essential to the war effort. At some stage Bill found the time to meet Mary Gladys Fairbank (known as Gladys) at Tekapo. Originally from Otago, she was a talented artist and sculptress, but also a person of the land. She was 28 and Bill was 43 when they married in Fairlie in 1923.

Their honeymoon was a trip over the Copland Pass, out to the West Coast and back to Mount Cook. Bill's young wife must have been fit and healthy to have made the fairly demanding journey. In between their busy times on the farm Bill managed to help guide people on the Tasman Glacier on occasion, while Gladys would take people for a short walk on the Ball Glacier and bring them back to the Ball Hut for a cup of tea.

The couple had four children, but Gilbert was the only one to become a farmer. The oldest son, Blake Macaulay, was born in 1924, his middle name a nod of respect to the Macaulay River that dominated their life while they were at Lilybank Station. A second son, Henry Albert Tasman, was born in 1926. His third name belonged to the mighty Tasman River

that flows into Lake Pukaki. The twins arrived in 1928: Myrtle Jean, known as Jean, and Gilbert Dionysius. (No one remembers why Dionysius became something of a family name, but since this is the Greek god of wine and agriculture, Gilbert is not complaining.)

It must have been challenging to care for four children born within four years, while living in a homestead sandwiched between the Macaulay and Godley rivers, both of which were prone to flooding. The Macaulay

was often unable to be forded, which meant the family would be completely cut off. However, Bill had also purchased a farm at Cave, about 35 kilometres from Timaru, so, after the children were born, they mainly lived there.

In 1929, after 14 years, Bill sold his share in Lilybank Station to his partner, Rex Malthus, who was now married, and moved back to his land at Cave, which was known as Pine Grove Farm. In 1935, at the age of 55, he purchased the 8500-hectare Ferintosh Station.

Ferintosh, originally known as Glenfield, had been subdivided from Glentanner in 1911. It had a series of owners before Bill, only one of them staying more than about two years. The Seymours have now been at Ferintosh for 80 years. This is a station that is spoilt for views, with Ben Ohau Range to the west, Aoraki/Mt Cook to the north and Lake Pukaki to the east. The homestead faces the lake and the ripple of the waves on the shore can often be heard from the house.

The original Glentanner homestead was situated about a kilometre north of Boundary Creek on what is now Ferintosh. The next Glentanner homestead was later built on the site it occupies today, but burned down on Christmas Day of 1949. Gilbert was at Ferintosh that day and was the first person called upon to help. They sought reinforcements, but it was too late to save it.

Bill, an expert marksman, established the Tasman Valley Miniature Rifle Club, basing the firing range at Ferintosh. He was also a committee member of the Mackenzie Country A&P Association for many years and won many prizes for his horses, ponies, vegetables, eggs, jam and butter. He was responsible for setting up the Highland dancing and bagpipe competitions, horse saddle trotting races and for establishing the Mackenzie Tartan Champion Ribbons gifted to winners of competitions at the Fairlie A&P Show.

Sadly, all was not well. Gladys contracted tuberculosis and was in poor health for much of her life as a mother. She died on 8 November 1944, aged only 45, and is buried in the Burkes Pass Cemetery. The family

ABOVE Ferintosh mailbox. MARY HOBBS
OPPOSITE Travellers near Birch Hill Station, heading towards Glentanner and Ferintosh Station. JACK ADAMSON

had been at Ferintosh for nine years. Gilbert was only 16 when he lost his mother, just as his father Bill had in 1896.

There was a great blow to the profitability of the station in 1952 when more than 1200 hectares of its most fertile flat country was lost with the first raising of Lake Pukaki. The freehold land Bill had bought to give his family security was also submerged. No compensation was paid. It was a tremendous loss to Bill, who had put an enormous amount of work into the property. He died in 1955.

When Gilbert took over the station in 1953, he ran approximately 3500 merinos and 150 head of cattle. These were boom years for farmers. The Korean War meant a great demand for wool and food, so prices were breaking previous records. Confidence was high.

As a young man Gilbert played rugby for the Pukaki Rugby Team and is probably its last surviving member. He also became a committee member of the Mackenzie Country A&P Association, and successfully carried on the family tradition of consistently winning prizes for his entries with sheep, wool and produce. In acknowledgement of his services, he was later made an honorary member. In 1965, Gilbert donated 153 larch trees for the building of extensions to Unwin Hut, now Unwin Lodge, at the entrance to Aoraki/Mount Cook National Park.

ABOVE Gilbert Seymour drafting merinos. GILBERT SEYMOUR COLLECTION
OPPOSITE Marion and Gilbert Seymour enjoy a walk in late summer. MARY HOBBS

The second raising of the lake, in 1976, took an additional 400 hectares of Ferintosh land, including 37 metres along the lake frontage. This time the homestead, the sheds, haybarns, the woolshed, outbuildings, workers' quarters and the cattle and sheep yards were all lost. There was compensation on this occasion, but it came nowhere close to full reimbursement.

In the earlier part of his life, Gilbert married his first wife, Jose Owen. They had five children aged between eight and 16 when, sadly, Jose died, aged only 49. It was the same year the lake was raised for a second time. It was an incredibly difficult time and Gilbert had a herculean task ahead of him. He knuckled down and, one step after another, began to rebuild.

After the lake was raised the government left the Mackenzie station holders another problem: they planted *Pinus contorta*, among other species, including larch and Douglas fir. Gilbert was told that the original intention was to plant the trees for 'scenic beauty', although in other areas it was considered they were planted in an attempt to stem erosion. It was probably thought that these trees were a positive choice because of their hardiness, but the decision devastated many stations, including Ferintosh. The pines grew much more prolifically in New Zealand than in their native North America, and have caused substantial loss of productive land in their inexorable, steady march across the landscape. They also make the soil more acidic and increase the fire danger to extremely high in summer.

Station holders have achieved some hard-won success in curbing the spread of the wilding pines by fencing areas that are able to be fenced, concentrating stock, improving pasture and grazing consistently, and by constant monitoring and action, but it costs a tremendous amount in lost production and is a negative gain.

Gilbert first met Marion on Birch Hill Station back in the 1950s, when they were both mustering. Their paths crossed again when Gilbert had been a widower for some years. Marion, who had three daughters, was very familiar with the outdoor life, having grown up on a farm and spent most of her working life on stations, including Lilybank. Skilled at mustering, and working with horses and dogs, she was no stranger to the harsh climate of the Mackenzie, or to hard work.

At Lilybank, Marion had often acted as a one-woman search and rescue team, locating people lost or trapped in the area. On several

occasions, she had the unenviable task of bringing out someone badly injured, by tractor and trailer, and once a person who had died – and all of this on her own. For these services over the years, Marion was later awarded a New Zealand Service Medal for her contribution to farming and the community.

Gilbert and Marion found each other great company and worked well together. They eventually married at St David's Church in Cave. It is very rare to see one without the other in the Mackenzie. They almost always attend local events and enter into things with great enthusiasm.

In the 1990s they had to contend with the rabbit plague, which had again become rampant. Most station holders were facing enormous bills each year for pest control. Some found it too hard to continue, but the Seymours forged on and the rabbit haemorrhagic disease (RHD) virus gave some respite.

The challenges with wilding pines continued. It has been heartbreaking for Marion and Gilbert to see the land gobbled up by the proliferation of pines. In a 2010 article for *New Zealand Geographic*, Dave Hansford, took a drive with Gilbert to see the forest of contorta that had spread over the slopes and asked if that was the plantation that had infested his farm. 'That *is* my farm,' Gilbert replied.[3]

Gilbert and Marion continue to work hard: shearing some of the few sheep they have left on the property, accommodating tree-cutters arriving to help quell the unruly wildings, helping with a local wedding, bottling fruit from their heirloom apricot trees, tackling the vegetable garden or, armed with chainsaws and loppers thrown onto the back of the Land Rover, dealing with more pines. They lease some of the land for cattle grazing and they are battling through the long tenure review process. Despite the challenges, and their increasing age, they are hardy souls who never take for granted this high country in which they live. As Marion says, 'It is where we are meant to be.'

OVERLEAF James Preston (wearing the tie) and his nephew J.E.P. Cameron up the Dobson Valley. CAMERON FAMILY COLLECTION

THE RACE FOR BENMORE STATION
(and Ben Ohau)

Way at the back of Fairlie, beneath the Great Divide,
Is the land found by Mackenzie, a million acres wide.
Last of the frontier country, lonely and apart,
A sea of golden tussock, with the iron in its heart.

Right on the farthest rim, hard by the mountain wall,
Stood a brace of mighty stations in the foremost rank of all.
One was named Ben Ohau, below the Ohau Range,
The other was called Benmore, vast, remote and strange.

They tell a famous story of how the land was won,
A cameo of history, a legend of the run.
Back in the 1850s, first of a rugged band,
Fraser and McMurdo came to this silent land.

Two hundred thousand acres, rough, untouched, untamed,
Awaiting the pioneer, undiscovered and unclaimed.
Both set their hearts on Benmore, the larger of the pair,
Though beautiful Ben Ohau was every bit as fair.

They settled the matter quickly, as men of action will,
A match-race for the choice, to the foot of a distant hill.
Each man was well-mounted, on a splendid rangy steed,
Tough and strong and game, built for guts and speed.

At the crack of Fraser's pistol, they flew out from the mark,
By the grandstand of the mountains, magnificent and stark.
Fighting for their heads, alive with speed and grace,
Bellies brushing tussock, they settled to the race.

Sod and gravel spurted beneath the flying pair,
And clouds of yellow dust, hung in the sunlit air.
Seven furlongs covered, and neither broke the line,
Though Fraser showed out slightly, coming to the nine.

The lead was just a whisker, and dearly was it bought,
The more he tried to stretch it, the more McMurdo fought.
Roaring up a gully they hit the rolling crest,
To face an ugly chasm, reaching to the west.

Too late to pull up short, too late to swing away,
The only path was forward, the only hope was pray.
Like blooded steeplechasers, in one almighty bound,
They cleared the yawning gulf, and both made good their ground.

Forward, ever forward, with barely slackened pace,
The drum-roll of their passage filled that silent place.
A clump of matagouri leaping into view,
Was ripped apart like paper, as they strongly barrelled through.

Fraser's hat went flying, his horse threw off a shoe,
McMurdo's saddle slipped, and his bridle snapped in two.
In and out of creek-beds, up and down the banks,
They drove the snorting chargers, with foam-caked bloody flanks.

Onward, onward, onward, over the stony plain,
Rash and reckless riding, a glittering prize to gain.
Fraser held his margin, half a length in front,
McMurdo dropping back, but still there in the hunt.

Rising in his stirrups he saw the winning post,
A bunch of stunted bushes, a hundred yards at most.
Driving in his spurs, he let the horse fly free,
Roaring, raving, cursing, prayers and profanity.

Like a greyhound from the traps, like a bullet from a gun,
McMurdo's mighty chestnut made its final run.
A dozen giant strides just buried Fraser's grey,
McMurdo hit the front, and McMurdo won the day.

As both men dropped exhausted to the hot and dusty ground,
While the horses shook and trembled, and breathed with desperate sound.
The ghosts of long dead horsemen rose from their long-filled graves,
And roars of acclamation rolled in echoing waves.

They crashed off the peaks and valleys, all the way to the Haast,
A torrent of ghostly applause, from the dim, lost world of the past.
Fraser heard the rumbling, and looked at the changing sky,
'A nor-west storm is coming Alex, the thunder's passing by.'[1]

Brian Barry, 2001

BEN OHAU

In about 1857 Hugh Fraser and Alex McMurdo were both on the hunt for suitable sheep country in the Mackenzie when they crossed the Ohau River and saw the Benmore Range before them. They decided to race each other to the Christchurch Land Office, after lunch. Then, while the billy was boiling, they agreed such an undertaking would be too rough on the horses, so settled for the finish line at a matagouri bush about a kilometre away. The winner would get the prize of Benmore and the other rider would get Ben Ohau. Hugh was pipped at the post and ended up with Ben Ohau. He and his brother Samuel applied for the Ben Ohau run on 20 April 1857, the same day that McMurdo put in his application for Benmore.[2]

Hugh Fraser was born in Inverness, Scotland in 1832 and arrived in Nelson in 1850, on the *Mariner*. When he married Jane Watson Thomson (or Thompson) on 21 March 1854 he was living at Beaver Station, Wairau. The couple eventually had six children.

With the assistance of Big Mick Radove, Hugh transported sheep from Nelson down to the Mackenzie. They were the first men to do so. Hugh managed various properties in the Nelson area before he and Alex McMurdo came upon Ben Ohau.[3]

A vast tract of land between the Pukaki and Ohau rivers, Ben Ohau was extended to include an additional 4855 hectares up in the ranges, amounting to an impressive 32, 520 hectares. Samuel managed the station.

Hazy spring day on Ben Ohau. MARY HOBBS

Little is known about the Frasers' time on Ben Ohau in those early days, though it is said that they grew barley and made their own whisky.[4] They eventually sold the station to William Ostler, Henry Dawson and Robert Campbell in 1870. William continued to manage Benmore Station until he bought his partners out four years later and moved to Ben Ohau.

When 18-year-old Emma Brignell Roberts of Melbourne married William Ostler on 14 July 1868, it signalled the beginning of their lives together in the Mackenzie Country. The couple initially settled at Benmore Station (then known as Ben More). It is perhaps easy to think that station life would have paled in comparison to Melbourne's social activities, but Emma's daughter, Helen Wilson, born in Oamaru in 1869, recalled her mother's stories of the fun they had. They would travel to dances at neighbouring stations on horseback with their finery in bandboxes that hung on their husbands' saddles.[5] Because they had to travel 100 kilometres, guests usually stayed for several days. The festivities included dancing, charades, sports and good conversation, with ample time to catch up on local news. There were picnics too, which were grand affairs, usually with a full tea service and abundant food carried in wicker baskets and served on the best English china.

When a gang of shearers travelled from shed to shed and wherever the shearers were at Christmas, a race meeting and sports were arranged. Everyone, including the owners, station hands, shearers and others in the district, entered their horses. Later, in the cool of the evening, they would clear away the wool-sorting tables, sweep the floors and dance in the woolshed, 'where Christmas fare was served according to old English traditions'. It was a time of affluence. For Helen, it seemed like a 'Golden Age … glimpses of good times that had passed'.[6] She did not recall her subsequent childhood at Ben Ohau in the same way.

Helen Wilson's autobiography, *My First Eighty Years*, published in 1950, gives a rare and valuable view of her life at Ben Ohau, where she grew up from the age of five. Helen warmly described her father as a 'huge, red-headed Yorkshireman of immense strength with … a sensitive and boyish nature', who was 'kindly and endearing'. He was often wistful for the familiar sights and sounds of the land of his birth. He 'let out a joyful

yell … and turned a somersault' when he saw his first English skylark in New Zealand.[7]

The Ben Ohau homestead, on Glen Lyon Road, near Twizel, was originally a primitive cob house that began as one large room, with a small room on each side. The walls were 60 centimetres thick and the roof was made of thatched snowgrass, with the chocolate brown roots facing outwards. Additional rooms were added as required in a straight line, with an 18-metre verandah along the front and the luxury of a fireplace in each room, and an entrance door to each room from the verandah.[8] This arrangement gave privacy, but also meant going outside for access in all weathers. A small hall led to a sizeable kitchen at the back and cob extensions from the kitchen provided living space for a married couple and a small dairy. The one exception to the cob material was a wooden room, with an iron roof, at one end of the verandah. Too hot in the summer and too cold in the winter to be used as a bedroom, this 'was called the bathroom, which meant that a round painted bath-tub was placed there, and water carried to it in pails'.[9]

To Helen, the wide landscape in which she grew up was 'a God-forsaken tract of land' as far as fertility was concerned, but those who lived there 'always spoke and acted as if belonging to the Mackenzie Country added cubits to their stature'.[10] Yet, perhaps to survive here, cubits were added to their stature, for it required extraordinary perseverance, and a certain indomitable optimism. Helen's rather dour view of the area may have been coloured by the tragedy her family met with there.

Yet she was not immune to the stunning beauty of the place. She described the frosted grass in winter, spangled with 'brilliant stars of red, blue and gold that seemed to stand higher than the snowy ground and to be flashing coloured signals to each other'. In winter long icicles reached from the roof of the verandah to the ground, completely glassing it in with 'a solid wall of rainbow colours, except for little vertical slits through which one could peep at the sun-lit world' before it collapsed in the heat of the sun later in the morning.[11]

There was no road to Ben Ohau in the 1870s, so the straightest line was taken, with the occasional guide from an old bullock track, while dodging the sharp spaniard shrubs and thorny matagouri. On one occasion, the Ostler family were returning home when they met with an accident, in

The old Ben Ohau homestead. CAMERON FAMILY COLLECTION

which their 'spirited horse … kicked the trap to pieces'.[12] They walked 11 kilometres to the Tekapo River ford-man's cottage, where they stayed the night. The next day William rode to the station and then returned in the dray to collect his family, Helen and her two siblings.

Despite the harshness of early pioneering life there were light-hearted moments, too. Emma used to love unwrapping monthly mail that contained precious copies of English magazines. No one, she said, 'could possibly feel isolated or out-of-the-world with picture papers… coming from the centre of things'. There in her kitchen, in 1875, she felt she was taken to the 'right to the scene of the action'.[13]

With farming going well, in 1876 Helen's parents also purchased a house in Timaru, but two years later there was a substantial snowstorm, followed by almost two months of hard frost. This made it impossible for the sheep to access any grass, even though they could see it beneath the ice. They died, 'feebly tapping the hard surface'. The entire Ben Ohau flock 'perished and had to be renewed'.[14]

ABOVE A welcome cuppa while haybaling. CAMERON FAMILY COLLECTION
OPPOSITE Sheep coming in for weaning draft. CAMERON FAMILY COLLECTION

Then came a slump in wool prices. A few years earlier farmers had achieved some of the best prices for wool but then just as suddenly they were plunged into the deep recession known as the Long Depression, which lasted from the late 1870s until the early 1890s.

Runholders were also affected by the Land Act of 1877, under which pastoral leases were for a term of 10 years and which offered deferred-payment schemes to encourage the settlers to take up smaller family farms.[15] As Helen records, the passing of this legislation so reduced the run's profits that William had to take his family back to Ben Ohau. According to her mother, the local MP Edward Wakefield wandered into the wrong parliamentary lobby, 'by an alcoholic accident', and the bill was carried by one vote. (Five years later, 'under the Land Act 1882, pastoral leases were extended from 10 to 21 years and the so-called perpetual lease was introduced'.[16] Sadly, this was too late for the Ostler family.)

In May 1879, at the close of a holiday, the rest of the family stayed with friends in Timaru while William returned to Ben Ohau to supervise the transport of wool bales to the market. The Friday before her father was due back, Helen looked out her window and saw one of the station hands riding slowly towards the house. She had a premonition that something of great significance had occurred.

The rider brought tragic news. On 11 May, William had been helping to manoeuvre wool bales across the Ohau River, in a cage on a wire rope, when one slipped and was about to roll into the river. With all his strength, he threw the bale hook he was holding into the bale and managed to save it. The men reported he spent a long time by the river drinking water. William walked slowly home, leading his horse, and went straight to bed, where he was found dead the next morning. The cause of death was later determined as internal bleeding – 'the rupture of a blood vessel close to the heart'.[17] In the words of the *Timaru Herald*, 'As a settler and private gentleman he was equally respected and esteemed, and his sad death, while apparently in robust health, at the comparatively early age of 45 years, will be deeply felt by a wide circle of friends'.[18]

William's family endured several bleak years of struggle, as the mortgagees of Ben Ohau foreclosed and put it up for auction. The station attracted little interest, owing to a rabbit plague, and Ben Ohau was passed in with no bids. Emma Ostler received nothing. Even though the

station did not sell, the heartless mortgagees sold the family's possessions, including Emma's beloved horse. Helen attended school in Timaru and boarded with a family while her mother returned to Ben Ohau the following year, hoping that a final settlement might make some provision for them. Things went from bad to worse when the mortgagees took over the property.[19] Emma disliked the young manager they chose, and the servants no longer took orders from their mistress.

There had been further tragedy at the station. In September 1879, only months after William's death, Mr and Mrs Morrison, who had been working at Ben Ohau, had resigned and, with two of their children, daughters aged 12 and 16, were returning to Oamaru on 19 September, taken in a wagonette by Ben Ohau manager William Stronach. Rather than using the flying fox to take his passengers across the Ohau River, as was usual, William continued through the dangerous and rocky water in the early morning darkness, with only a man, who had crossed on the flying fox, endeavouring to guide them in the direction of the safest ford. The vehicle's wheels sank into a deep hole, the horses tried to bolt and the wagonette capsized. The manager caught one of the young girls, and he and Mr Morrison escaped to the bank, but Mrs Morrison and the older daughter, Ann, were swept down the river and drowned.[20] They were buried high on the bank, close to where the accident occurred, and close to the Ruataniwha Rowing Course, where their graves remain. The women of the Mackenzie later placed a headstone on the shared grave in memory of the woman and her daughter.

Realising there was little to keep her at the station, and facing the formidable challenge of keeping her family together, Emma Ostler returned to Timaru, where she gave dance and art classes. There was a life insurance payment of £1000 but Emma worked so she could save this money for her children's education. After moving to Levin in order to take part in a land ballot in the area, in 1888 she won an 8-hectare section, which she and Helen developed.

Ostler remains a well-known name in this part of the high country. A fault line on the south side of Twizel is known as the Ostler Fault and nearby is Ostler Road. The southernmost in the chain of hills behind Ben Ohau homestead is named Mount Ostler.

In the late 1870s, a young woman named Jane Honour was playing croquet among the flax bushes near Oamaru, on the east coast of the South Island. Also playing that day was Mrs Sutherland, whose husband, Duncan, managed Omarama Station. She invited Jane to visit but she could not afford such a journey. Mrs Sutherland perhaps guessed that funds were short, so later wrote to Jane and suggested that she might like to become the governess for the family of Benmore manager Thomas Middleton.[21]

Today we think nothing of a quick trip from Oamaru to Omarama but in 1880 Jane was embarking on an adventure into the great unknown. Her long journey, on a hot, dusty day, took her to Omarama, where Mrs Sutherland and her niece had laid out a generous station tea of cold mutton, eggs and scones. It was now 7 p.m., the sun was still hot and everywhere she looked there seemed to be only a landscape of burnt, dry tussock. Then the Middletons arrived to take her on the final stage of her journey to Benmore.

There Jane was delighted to find the homestead verandah heavily laden with honeysuckle in full bloom, reminding her of her childhood home in England. She enjoyed her time with the Middletons and their seven children, who had an ear for music, combined with a natural

Sheep on Ben Ohau after crutching. CAMERON FAMILY COLLECTION

intelligence and positive outlook. When three-year-old Mary (Mopey) fractured her leg it was decided that Jane should ride to Omarama to ring the doctor. He could meet the train at Kurow and tend to Mopey there. Jane made the trip and stayed one night at Kurow before making her way back to Omarama, only to find that all the men and horses were away mustering and there was no horse available for her to return. Ben Ohau manager William Stronach was at the hotel. He had ridden in that morning with a friend, who was about to catch the coach, so a spare horse had unexpectedly become available. He was happy to escort the young governess back to Benmore. Jane remembered it as a 'momentous ride'. She would never forget the 'waning light, the tussocky road, the winding, straggling stream'.

The rest of the year was very happy for Jane. There were horse races around a lagoon at the back of the house and skating there in winter. Those who could not skate were also included, for the blacksmith attached runners to chairs and they were drawn around the ice on these. Fires were lit and there were copious amounts of hot tea, lashings of good food and easy laughter, accompanied by the hoot of moreporks. Jane recalled, too, the sharp, crisp frost, with the 'spear grass golden tipped and the rocks sparkling'.

William Stronach and Jane were married at St Luke's in Oamaru the following year, 1881. The bride wore a gown of white merino with an inset of white satin, combined with a beautiful skirt of old Irish lace. After honeymooning in Dunedin, Jane began her life on Ben Ohau.

One of the greatest challenges was finding sufficient wood to keep warm in the winter. There was no native bush, except for odd pockets in the gorges and by the lakeside and at the head of the lake. The men began cutting wood at the head of Lake Ohau in early summer so enough was stacked and dried for the winter, after being rafted down the lake and carted to the homestead. The wood supply was supplemented by nearby peat, which was cut in spring, stacked and dried through the summer and stored close to the house. Three tonnes of coal for the blacksmith's forge was also brought in each year, along with other supplies. Wool was carted back to Oamaru on the return trip.

Jane loved her life in the Mackenzie. Although she found the frosts severe, they did not stop her from gazing at the brilliance of the starry

and their trip back on foot was rough and long. The horses were eventually located and they rode back to camp very tired.

When the owner of Waitangi Station, Robert Turnbull Miller, came to visit Ben Ohau for a week he invited Jane and William to a party. Would they come? 'But of course,' said Jane, 'we must!' They set off at about 9 a.m. in a buggy, wrapped up in possum rugs to fend off the biting wind. More possum rugs were laid in the front for their baby. Snowshoes were also tucked in. As usual, when travelling south, the first hurdle was the flying fox at the Ohau River. They were pleased to get over it in about two hours. They called in at Benmore, and had lunch at Omarama with the Sutherlands, who were also about to set off for the party. They boarded a boat to cross the Waitaki, finally arriving at Waitangi homestead, where they were made very welcome. Jane was particularly touched that Robert Miller, a bachelor, had arranged for a tiny bed to be made up in the bottom drawer of an old chest in their room for their baby. After dinner they danced the night away.

Jane also remembered travelling up to Lake Ohau Station with her husband, their two babies, and a nursemaid. There was a mishap with the flying fox, and all the baby clothes disappeared downstream. Jane was upset and unsure of what to do, but the nursemaid, Ada, was of great comfort. She said, 'Oh, let's go. I'll manage somehow about their clothes'. So off they went.

No sooner had they arrived at the station than Jane ventured off on horseback with her friend, Mary Maitland. They set off at around 4 a.m. and returned for breakfast. With a chop in one hand and a 'huge chunk of bread' in the other, they went off again, exploring on horseback, riding for miles. They enjoyed it all so much that they stayed for a fortnight.

Jane and William's time on Ben Ohau Station came to a close. It is not known where they moved on to, but Jane's memoirs leave no doubt that Ben Ohau and the wild spaces of the Mackenzie with its big skies always remained close to her heart.

The Long Depression led to many runholders either leaving their land or yielding their properties to loan companies. Rabbits had also become a massive problem. Between 1877 and 1884, 75 Otago runs were abandoned because of the rabbits.[22] In 1889, when the Canterbury runs were up for renewal and were reoffered, there were no bids for Ben Ohau,

nights, and she loved the seasonal changes, especially spring, which brought the beauty of warmer days when gentian flowers of the brightest blue could be found near creekbeds. Snowberries grew in great profusion on the hills, and once she found the hillside white with Mount Cook lilies.

As with most stations, visitors regularly passed through. Jane took advantage of this by going tramping with them as often as she could. On one occasion, Herbert Maitland, the government surveyor, visited with his wife, Mary, and they enjoyed many lakeside picnics. At one point they tied their horses to tussocks and went off to explore, only to find that the animals had eaten the tussock and vanished. A nor'wester had sprung up,

ABOVE Simon Cameron goes for a ride with Morris Snuchell, the last of the old rabbiters. CAMERON FAMILY COLLECTION
OPPOSITE Simon Cameron's father, Jack, takes an afternoon nap on the family swing. CAMERON FAMILY COLLECTION

so it was retained by the mortgage company until James Henry Preston purchased it in 1891. He also held the leases of Haldon and Black Forest stations, and had assisted his brother-in-law onto Lilybank Station, so he was stretched thin.

The rabbit plague was severely affecting all the stations, as the animals ate their way through the feed intended for the sheep. According to local lore, the trouble with rabbits in the Mackenzie began when a bridge was put across the Ohau River. The rabbits must have thought the bridge was built for them, as they put it to good use, swarming over it from Otago and into South Canterbury, where they bred in great numbers.

In the late 1880s, a 128-kilometre fence stretching from Aoraki/Mount Cook to Kurow was erected to prevent rabbits spreading from Otago into South Canterbury. Parts of it can still be seen on the Mount Cook Road. But the rabbits still made their way through. It was decided that stoats, weasels and ferrets were the answer to the problem and despite vociferous protests that they would make native birds extinct, breeding stations were established and thousands were released. It made little difference to the rabbit problem, but a great deal of difference to the dawn chorus.

A commercial industry was started in an attempt to control the rabbits. By 1893, approximately 17 million rabbit skins had been sent to England and exports peaked in 1924 at around 20 million. There was a view, however, that poisoning the rabbits and not using the meat was wasteful and a missed exporting opportunity, so the animals were killed cleanly and several meat-preserving plants were set up to can the meat,

but the enterprise failed to make much impression on rabbit numbers. Exports of frozen rabbit carcasses were more successful: 6.5 million were sent in 1900, almost all of them from Otago and Southland.[23]

After the combined devastation of the 1895 snowstorm and the rabbit plague, James mentioned to his nephew, John Edward Preston Cameron, who had grown up on Aviemore Station, that he would have to sell Ben Ohau. John, who had been working as a station hand at Benmore, and later managing Ben Ohau, asked if he could buy it. He took over the lease in 1897 and Ben Ohau has remained in the Cameron family since. After John married in 1903, he and his family lived on a property at Linton, west of Timaru, and John would travel to the station by horseback each fortnight to liaise with the manager. The family were also on the station for shearing, weaning lambs and holidays. During the summer they would live on the verandah of the homestead and simply roll down a canvas for privacy. They also had a kitchen made at one end of the verandah.

John Cameron, too, had his share of unforeseen challenges, chief of which was that the station seemed to disappear before his eyes. In 1911 the government brought in boundary changes that reduced the station from 32,520 to 23,180 hectares. That is a considerable amount from a property that requires large areas of land to remain viable, owing to the poor quality soil and the correspondingly small number of sheep to the hectare. In 1918 the government subdivided the high country stations again, so soldiers returning from the war would have an opportunity to go into a ballot to obtain a farm. In what was known as the Soldier Settlement Scheme another 16,580 hectares was sliced off Ben Ohau, after which it covered 6600 hectares. Over the 17 years the Cameron family owned the leasehold, they had made substantial improvements to the station, but they were not permitted even to choose which block they would prefer to retain, so their improved area was on the market as well, and there was nothing they could do about it.

The property was eventually divided into four separate runs: Omahau, Ruataniwha, Bendrose and the Ben Ohau homestead block of around 6500 hectares, which was eventually allocated to the Cameron

Joan Cameron delivers afternoon tea in the family Chevy to the harvesters. CAMERON FAMILY COLLECTION

family, as well as a freehold block of 90 hectares given as a small token of compensation.

Despite the major blow, John focused on developing a merino stud. In 1927 he built an outstanding sheepshed of heart rimu, with the intention of housing his stud sheep. But the 1929 Wall Street crash, and the subsequent depression, meant there was no demand for stud sheep, so the shed was used to shelter recently shorn sheep. Conditions gradually improved, though, and in the succeeding years, John won prizes in New Zealand and Australia for his merinos. John died in 1950 while out droving. He would have been very proud to see his grandson, Simon, and his wife Priscilla, awarded international prizes in fleece quality, through the use of his beloved shed.

John Cameron's son, also John, but known as Jack, came up to manage Ben Ohau for his father in 1936. He was 17. When he brought his wife Joan (née Bussell) home to the station in 1942, conditions were primitive, with no power and no inside toilet. Before a copper arrived some years later, Joan washed the children's nappies by hand in the nearby Fraser Stream.

Jack used to throw a bit of kerosene down the long-drop once in a while, just to keep the smell down. One day a friend of the family, a judge, as it happened, went to the toilet, lit a smoke and innocently dropped it down. Boom! Out leapt the judge with part of his bottom singed, sure the outhouse had been struck by lightning. Everyone agreed that nothing had ever unseated a judge quite as quickly. The fire was smothered with corn sacks, but Joan found it difficult to assist because she was gripped by helpless laughter. Years later, with the invention of the barbecue, Jack could be heard commenting that with the cooking done outside and the toilet now inside, what would be next?

Rabbits remained a problem, with every nibble turning the place into a desert. Jack reduced the population by hiring eight rabbiters, who sold the meat and skins. The government then established the Rabbit Board, which proved an effective tool. Jack was a strong supporter and from 1947 to 1991 served on the Lake Pukaki Rabbit Board, whose territory ranged between the Ohau and Pukaki rivers. He then became chairman of the South Island Rabbit Board, travelling around 60,000 kilometres each year in his bid to keep the rabbits under control. To keep costs down, he never

put in a request to be compensated for the mileage. They had good results between 1947 and the 1970s, using aerial poisoning and 1080. Rabbiters also worked the land, but the cost of maintaining any progress was substantial because the rabbits bred so prolifically.

Jack also became a member of the local council, which extended from Kurow to the Rangitata. One day he returned home from Blenheim, where he had been at a meeting, to find seven-year-old Simon doubled up with an acute stomach ache. After one look at his son, he diagnosed appendicitis and he and Joan drove Simon, at great speed, straight to Timaru Hospital. He was immediately put into theatre and as the surgeon opened him up, his appendix burst. It was not the only mercy dash that kind-hearted Jack made to Timaru: he acted as an impromptu ambulance service when required, as he knew the primitive roads well, and could drive fast.

Jack doubled the number of sheep and tripled the cattle on the station by putting in extra water races for stock, and working the land to make it more fertile. Yet, like his father, Jack was concerned about the continual government reduction of the station's viability through land appropriation. To protect it from further land grabs he vigorously sought

ABOVE A family snap of the dam works on Ben Ohau. CAMERON FAMILY COLLECTION
OPPOSITE Harvesting oats. CAMERON FAMILY COLLECTION

to freehold it, but his application was turned down. Unknown to Jack, the government was about to create a series of dams for hydro-electricity and Ben Ohau was one of the stations in the firing line.

From 1967 to 1983 the government took further chunks of high country land to construct canals as part of the series of hydro-electric dams created in the area. Ben Ohau was one of many stations to lose some of its most fertile land. An additional 800 hectares of premium farmland was appropriated. The compensation was a minuscule $32,000. Between 1897 and 1977 the station was reduced from 32,520 to just 4210 hectares, which, on relatively poor soil, was barely enough to be viable.[24] Similar cuts occurred elsewhere, and brought many high country stations in the district to the brink.

Jack found it 'quite a traumatic thing … to have them here taking our land'. When the work was completed, half of the station was above the canal and half of it below, with only one access bridge. A lot of extra work was required to get stock up and down for shearing and during mustering. 'It was quite a worry for us while it was happening as we were never sure what else we would lose, and would we even have a farm left at the end? Our livelihood was on the line.'[25]

After the 'initial shock of seeing people everywhere',[26] Joan Cameron looked on the positive side. She enjoyed not having to travel several hours for supplies, as the town of Twizel was built (on land that originally belonged to Ben Ohau) to cater for those who worked on the hydro scheme. A local shopping centre sprang up and there were sealed roads, and schools for the children.

Born in 1920, Joan had grown up in Fairlie where her parents, Mr and Mrs Thomas Bussell, owned a large drapery shop that catered for the country township and surrounding stations. During the Second World War, as part of the war effort, Joan joined others in learning to cook for large numbers of people, in case things became worse in the Pacific and women were later required to cater for large numbers of soldiers. As part of this training, Joan cooked for nurses at Timaru Hospital. It was an experience she was grateful for when she later became the wife of a station owner.

There was no reticulated power at the homestead until 1958, although from the early 1900s a waterwheel and diesel generator plant had been installed for house lights.

The days were long, but neighbours helped each other and socialised together. A billiard room at nearby Rhoborough Downs was pressed into service as a dance floor and the district would get together for a dance. Musters were also a great opportunity to socialise. Joan would pack her three children, Jeanette, Ailsa and Simon, in the car and join the muster. Houses were left unlocked and people could pop in, knowing there would always be a warm welcome.

After school, Simon became involved in an International Agricultural Exchange programme and learned more about farming techniques in the United States, Canada and Denmark. In 1976 he became a partner in the station. Jeanette, who married Tim Riley (originally from Timaru Creek and Dingle stations), and Ailsa, who married plant scientist Dr Warwick Scott, both have land at Ben Ohau and enjoy returning to the place they love.

Although busy, Simon managed to escape occasionally to Queenstown. In 1984, he was there skiing and met New Zealand nurse Priscilla Smith, who was working as a ski-hostess at Coronet Peak. Priscilla was enjoying the welcome change from her high-powered and exciting work as a registered nurse in a London Coronary-Thoracic Unit. Eight months later she found herself married and on a 5000-hectare station without a patient in sight. Later, she became the local district nurse, and then a mother, as well as helping Simon on the station and providing food for sub-contractors.

In Simon's father's day, most farmers were encouraged to invest heavily in new technology, which saved on labour costs and helped to improve production, but, combined with the enormous cost of battling the rabbit problem, also dramatically increased mortgages. This was manageable until 1984, when the government stopped farm subsidies, creating an excess of debt, which made it hard for high country stations to stay afloat. The burden of debt enforced changes. It was either get out or innovate around the challenges, which, at times, looked insurmountable.

But the government had not finished appropriating land. By the completion of the hydro work in 1982, Ben Ohau was reduced by a further

ABOVE Merinos wait their turn to be shorn. MARY HOBBS
OPPOSITE Simon Cameron with some of his beloved dogs. MARY HOBBS

1200 acres. It is easy to understand why the Camerons were anxious to freehold. To do this, they had to go through the tenure review process, and were the first station holders to apply.

In 2001, Ben Ohau was officially the first station to become freehold under the Crown Pastoral Land Act of 1998, but not before DOC chose a further 1516 hectares of very special land. Jack was upset about what he saw as a lack of acknowledgement for the sensitive way these areas had been protected, but a portion of the station is now a protected wetland area designated as conservation estate, which works well for both parties.

After an Australian sheep classer, Gordy McMaster, invited Simon to visit Australia to look at a new way of doing things, Simon and Priscilla decided to take the plunge on producing world-class merino fleece. The project involved hand-feeding merinos inside a shed, with the sheep enjoying brief excursions outside for exercise. It was a great leap of faith, as the initial investment in the finest quality sheep and the constant attention came at substantial extra cost in time and money, but the huge commitment paid off. Simon and Priscilla won the Loro Piana New Zealand Record Bale Trophy in 2001. Aside from an excellent wool price, this earned them a five-star 10-day holiday in Italy, and time with the Loro Piana family. Ben Ohau won this award five times. The record

bale was a delicate 12.0 microns and was classed finer than cashmere. Another outstanding award was the Ermenegildo Zegna Vellus Aureum International Trophy for ultrafine wool in 2008. The record bale of 10.8-micron fleece came in at 1.47 kilograms. The prize was the weight of the winning fleece paid in gold, which was equivalent to the value of $50,000. This prize money was set aside to invest in irrigation.

At this moment someone, somewhere in the world, is probably wearing a fine suit cut from some of the highest quality merino that has ever been produced. Finer than cashmere, it is so rare that, when Simon and Priscilla were involved, only 40 garments were made from one bale in any one year. The merino wool attracted up to $150,000 for a premium bale. Unfortunately the explosion of cheap synthetic fabric on the market caused the wool prices to dive and eventually Simon and Priscilla phased out of that market.

There were many other innovations, including a brief period with goats that produced the finest mohair. They sold those at the top of the

market. Another inspired idea was inviting Peter Jackson to use the station for some of the major scenes in his *Lord of the Rings* trilogy. The Battle of the Pelennor Fields was fought on Ben Ohau and tours of the area are available. There is also an airstrip on the station where sightseeing flights land, a track where major car companies test tyres and make ads, and there is now cottage-stay accommodation.

The old cob cottage has long since gone, burned down by a disgruntled shearer in Simon's grandfather's day, but the current homestead, now over 100 years old, sits easily on the land. The dairy that Helen Wilson mentioned in her book still stands, along with the coal/peat shed, the storeroom and the old meat safe. The old woolshed remains in good use. Off to one side is a small kitchenette where a framed certificate graces the wall, on a casual slant. It was awarded to 'J. Cameron: A Gold Medal for Crossbred Ewe and Hogget Wools (in fleece) in the Panama Pacific International Exposition, San Francisco, 1904–1915'.

Most high country station runholders have many other talents and Simon, in addition to playing a 12-string guitar, is also a proficient painter. Priscilla worked for 16 years as the district nurse. With her warm smile and caring nature, it would be hard to find anyone more suited. She was a volunteer for St John for five years, and is now on the St John ambulance committee. These days she is still busy helping Simon on the station, and providing food on call for hungry workers. As a devoted mum, she keeps up with the activities of their two daughters, Janie and Sarah-Rose (Tiggy). She also runs the cottage-stay that has recently been placed on the property.

As for the future, the Camerons are turning their eye towards holistic farming, with the main focus on the natural cycle of the land and its relationship with the climate. To ensure the station remains viable they will not run dairy but will invest in irrigation to provide stock feed. They are not afraid to try new things if they make sense, and whatever direction they take, they are passionate about creating high-quality products that tell a story, while continuing to improve the land for future generations to nurture and enjoy.

ABOVE The garden at Ben Ohau. MARY HOBBS
OPPOSITE Priscilla, Simon and Tiggy Cameron on the verandah at the Ben Ohau homestead. MARY HOBBS
OVERLEAF The Ohau Canal with the Ben Ohau Range in the distance. MARY HOBBS

SIMONS HILL

In the summer of 1911 Evelyn Hosken stood in the middle of a vista of endless tussock and looked about in dismay. No matter where she cast her eye, as far as she could see there was nothing, nothing but this empty, barren landscape, broken only by the odd boulder. She felt an overwhelming sense of disappointment. In fact, she felt quite ill as she remembered that she and her husband had just signed an agreement to live here, in this place, for a minimum of five years. At that moment, to 24-year-old Evelyn, it felt more like a prison sentence. The ink was barely dry on the document. What had they done? There were no neighbours for miles, and although they had left their home in Ashburton just two days ago to visit this place, she already felt indescribably homesick. While these unwelcome thoughts crowded into her mind, her husband William, a carpenter by trade, and her brother, a farmer, had wandered off to look about the property.[1]

The Mackenzie Country stations were subdivided into smaller blocks in 1911 and Evelyn and William, who had married on 3 March 1907, had entered the ballot for a run. What they later named Simons Hill had been subdivided from Simons Pass and covered a land area of 6475 hectares and a forest reserve of a further 180 hectares. The east boundary was the Maryburn and Tekapo rivers, and the north boundary was the road to Mount Cook. The land ran to the junction of the Tekapo and Pukaki rivers. In her book, *Life on a Five Pound Note*, Evelyn recalls that, in their time, the station carried around 5000 sheep.

Looking towards Simons Hill Station from Pukaki Airport. MARY HOBBS

to maintain the 128-kilometre rabbit-proof fence that stretched from Mount Cook to Kurow, so Evelyn, her husband and brother set out to find it. As the buggy rounded a bend on the track they suddenly seemed to enter a different world, of green paddocks and a row of willow trees, 'all evenly trimmed by the horses which would pick off every leaf within reach'.[2] A cottage peeped out from behind a sweet-smelling hedge of lilac. There was also an orchard at the back, the trees so heavily laden with cherries, plums and pears that their branches scraped the ground.

Mr and Mrs Smart, an older couple, greeted them warmly: 'Good-day, are you the lucky people who have drawn this run?'[3] The Hoskens were ushered inside like old, long-expected friends. Over 50 years later, this hospitable greeting, the invitation to stay the night and the following convivial conversation and hot food, remained in Evelyn's mind as an unforgettable experience, and the pivotal moment when she began to see the more positive aspects of their great adventure. In the dim candlelight, as Evelyn watched Mrs Smart and her daughter preparing more food for their unexpected guests, she realised how much extra work was involved. For the rest of her life, she always kindly carried a loaf of fresh bread and a basket of extra food with her whenever she visited anyone in the country.

The Hoskens returned to Ashburton, where they sold their beloved home – there was not even a house on Simons Hill – and sadly farewelled the rest of the family. Evelyn remembered a friend arriving one day as she morosely contemplated their departure. She asked her if she thought there would be any birds up at Simons Hill, to which Mrs Walker replied, 'Of course there will be, and the same sun and moon as shines on you here will shine on you up there. So get out of the rut, my girl, go, and may God's blessing go with you both.'[4] Another friend gave Evelyn the precious gift of teaching her how to make bread. This was an essential skill, as there were no cars where the Hoskens were going and they had to order in supplies that would last for a year. Goods came out by horse and wagon and wool would be loaded for the trip back to the coast.

Evelyn made her first order of provisions for the year in Fairlie, with Mr Bateman of the Farmers' Co-op. She could not believe the quantities she had to order: 'Six 200lb [90-kilogram] sacks of flour, twelve 56lb [25-kilogram] bags of sugar, a 50lb [22-kilogram] chest of tea, rice, oatmeal, salt, etc, all in 25lb [11-kilogram] bags and smaller goods and tinned

The main prerequisites for an applicant for the land were an interview with the Land Board, a promise to live on whatever run was allocated for five years, a family and some experience of life in the country. Evelyn had grown up on a farm, they had a one-year-old son and they agreed to stay for five years.

The government had allocated a house to the man who was employed

products all worked out proportionately.'[5] She then visited Bussell's drapery store, which stocked a wide range of goods, including linoleum, bedding, curtains and all manner of items required for living in the high country. Tommy Bussell's kind and understanding manner impressed Evelyn, as he explained the necessity for such things as large blankets for men who would spend unplanned nights at the station. This was the first of countless orders Evelyn made from Tommy. He never walked around the long counter but instead took a short cut by sitting on it and swinging his legs over the other side. He employed James Craig as a travelling representative who visited each of the high country stations. Everyone stopped work when James arrived as he not only brought longed-for goods, but also the local gossip and news.

The first order of business at Simons Hill was to build a home. It took an inordinate amount of effort to get the building supplies, which had to be carted in by wagon. William's skill as a carpenter was put to good use in building their homestead, the woolshed, storeroom and other implement sheds. He first knocked together a three-room corrugated iron shed in which the family lived while he built their home. It was later converted into an implement shed.

While they were camped out in the shed, Evelyn rode, side-saddle, eight kilometres to the orchard, picked fruit and carried it back in tins on horseback. Back home she made jam over an open fire, with the one saucepan they owned. There were no jars, so Evelyn's brother improvised by cutting beer bottles to the required size and making a ring from wire used for fencing. A handle was attached so Evelyn could hold the ring over the fire. When it was hot enough she placed it over the top of the bottle. When she plunged the bottle, with wire attached, into cold water the top of the bottle would break off in a clean cut, which made a jar. The jars were filed to smooth the edges, cleaned, and filled with preserves. The jam was put to good use, but perhaps its most instantaneous effect was the feeling of comfort and satisfaction Evelyn had whenever she looked at the plentiful jars of jelly and jam all lined up in her shed.

The first lights at the homestead were candles, often homemade, and kerosene lamps. The lamps required a regular clean, which added to the daily tasks. Evelyn cooked early breakfasts for the family and others working on the station. She held a candle in one hand while turning the chops over with the other. Eventually a small battery plant was installed and was sufficient for the homestead to have electric light, but that was pretty much it until around 1959, when the hydro scheme brought electricity. She had three children to take care of as well.

Simons Hill was the first home in the Mackenzie to have hot water inside, though that came with great risk, because of the danger of being caught by a random freeze, causing the pipes to burst. Despite draining the pipes in winter, they were caught out a few times, which meant ripping down walls to mend the pipes, as well as drying out the area. In one particularly cold winter the water wasn't running at all, so they had to melt snow until it became warmer. On another 'frosty' morning, probably when the mercury had hit around -15°C, Evelyn was shocked to find that her treasured bottled fruit was still standing in the storeroom, but surrounded by shattered glass. Some of the young chickens had frozen on their perch that night and lost their feet, so had to be destroyed, and eggs that had been left out overnight had frozen.

Perhaps out of all the incidents occurring with frosts in the high country, it was the rescue of some puppies that Evelyn most clearly remembered. The men had gone out at 2.30 a.m. on early muster and Evelyn and Mary, a young girl helping out on the station, went to milk the cows at about 8.30. They found the stable door ajar, where some puppies, just a few days old, had been with their mother, a working sheepdog. She had gone and the puppies were frozen into a hard block of ice. It was a ghastly sight. Evelyn quickly scooped them into her apron and ran into the house, where she and Mary immersed them in warm water, over and over again. The place was a mess with water everywhere, but about two hours later their efforts were rewarded when they felt faint movement and heard some tiny squeaks. With renewed vigour they continued until, to their delight, they had five contented puppies. Apparently their mother had heard the men leaving for muster and, thinking her job was with them had gone to assist, refusing orders to return home. She came back with the men and resumed her motherly duties.

Despite the difficulties in procuring building supplies, the Hoskens' home eventually became well established, although a new oven was

The view from Simons Hill. MARY HOBBS

148

needed, which meant a long trip to Christchurch to chose one, then a long trip back, and a wait of many weeks for its arrival. William told Evelyn to choose the range she wanted and she was thrilled to find the perfect one. The prized purchase was sent to Fairlie by rail, then by wagon to Simons Hill. When it was finally unloaded it was found to be the wrong one. Back the oven went. The correct one arrived at long last, and Evelyn cooked and baked on it for decades, until, that is, the day the house caught on fire.

That particular day was very windy. To anyone in the high country, 'very windy' means the trees in the shelterbelts bending at crazy angles, and sometimes breaking in half, with gales shaking the house. Evelyn's daughter, and a girl working for them, were ironing. Starching and ironing shirts, dresses and a great deal of table and bed linen was a long, weekly job. The irons had to be heated on top of the range, so it was stoked up and pumping out a lot of heat. Evelyn thought she heard a roar, slightly more perhaps than the wind. She looked about her: was that a slight wisp of smoke coming from beneath the skirting boards? Yes, there was another wisp. Work carried on but Evelyn was disconcerted enough to begin filling the bath and all containers to hand with water just in case there was a fire at the back of the range she could not see.

William, out in the woolshed, just happened to glance up when, to his horror, he saw thick cumulus smoke billowing under the eaves of the house. He took off. By the time he reached the house, flames had fanned out into the dining room, which was situated behind the range. At first there had been a tiny pinprick of light, as though from a fire, and in an instant it had reached the ceiling. Its speed was frightening. The walls were lined with scrim and paper, which acted like kerosene to the flames.

William frantically tore down the wall where the fire had broken out and saw a hole in the back of the range that had caused the house studs to catch fire. Their daughter quickly climbed up into the manhole and looked down, finding thick smoke pouring out through the rafters. They drenched the hot studs with copious buckets of water until, finally, the timber was black, charred and exuding an acrid smoke. The family were buoyed by the knowledge they had managed to avert a major disaster in

The original homestead on Simons Hill. MARY HOBBS

the nick of time. There was water and soot everywhere, and relief in tears, but they cleaned up, and, to their delight, found 'a huge leg of mutton beautifully simmering in the roasting dish, not a bit the worse for the mess and upheaval all around'.[6] Evelyn's beloved oven had to be removed and replaced, though, until her dying day, that old Atlas range held a special place in her heart.

There were many swaggers travelling the roads in the early 1900s, and it was up to the station holder's wife to provide a lunch and fill their tea billy. Evelyn's sister was alone in the house one day when a swagger arrived for food. She said she would bring some to him and went to close the door, but he barred it with his foot. Without hesitation she bravely reached for the revolver from a nearby shelf and told him to go or she would shoot him. He left. She confessed she had been terrified for, despite her being a crack shot, the revolver was not loaded.

Harvesters and shearers visited Simons Hill every season and, although there was a married couple assisting the family, and the shearers brought a cook, towards the end of one season the latter stormed off on a drinking binge, which meant Evelyn had to step into the breach. There were quite a few mouths to feed and because the shearers' cookhouse was out by the shearing shed, meals were ferried quite a distance, several times a day. Then it rained. No shearing, but the shearers had to wait it out, and Evelyn was convinced they ate more when they were resting. The harvesters were there at the same time and they had to be catered for as well.

Evelyn came from a farming family near Timaru, where her mother was frequently called upon to deliver babies and help nurse others in isolated cob cottages scattered throughout the district. There were few neighbours, so everyone helped as best they could. For Evelyn at Simons Hill, there was no medical help nearby, bad roads and, of course, no telephone. Initially, the idea of an emergency worried her, but she selected Professor Kirk's book on home treatment, and another book of a similar title, by a Professor Kuhne, absorbed the information and immediately felt more capable. As she learned, a basic principle was that whatever treatment she gave 'had to be comforting. If it was upsetting in any way, I knew the treatment was not being given correctly'.[7]

Over the years, Evelyn had a wide variety of illnesses to tend to. Rabbiters came in from camp occasionally, one with a bad case of neuralgia, to which she applied warm compresses. There was no relief, so she tried cold compresses. This worked and the man fell into a deep relaxing sleep, which was a vast improvement from his arrival, when he was in such acute distress that he had threatened to shoot himself.

Her greatest achievement in home treatment was when her husband developed a case of blood poisoning from a splinter. William had removed the splinter and carried on with wool classing, thinking nothing of it, but he awoke during the night with a throbbing pain in his finger. He worked the following day, but his symptoms became worse that evening. The pain intensified and large lumps appeared under his arms. Evelyn should have rushed him to the doctor at that point, but instead she turned to Professor Kirk and administered steam baths and all manner of other treatments. It took her two weeks of dedicated work but she eventually cured the finger.

On another occasion, during harvesting, one man was sent to the nearby creek for water. As he bent down to fill the bucket, he saw an old kerosene tin submerged. Curiosity got the better of him, and he pulled it out of the water and took a look inside, only to find a syrup tin fitted with a tight lid. The temptation was too much, so off came the lid. Inside were 'what looked like sticks of lolly', so he popped one into his pocket, intending to ask his mates if they had any idea what it was. He was so busy when he returned that it quickly slipped his mind – until he hopped up onto the hay and found himself surrounded by fire. He felt heat down his leg and put his hand in his pocket: it 'became covered with this toffee like substance which soon began its deadly work of burning into his flesh'.[8] Luckily the others recognised that the 'lolly' was a stick of phosphorus and they wasted no time in stripping him of his clothes and putting out the flames. This all happened about 5 kilometres from the homestead, and the patient was transferred there for Evelyn to nurse. She sponged him down and dressed his wounds. After he ate, she left him for the evening, in good spirits, quite confident he would make a rapid recovery. Evelyn was aghast to find the burns were much worse the next morning as the phosphorus had continued to burn its way into his flesh overnight. The bus from the Hermitage collected him the next day and he was deposited at Timaru Hospital, where he had skin grafts to repair the damage. He eventually made a full recovery.

There are many stories of Evelyn's ministrations, all of which required skill and confidence and included setting the fractured leg of a lamb, as well as stitching and bandaging it and applying a splint. The lamb made a complete recovery. On another occasion Evelyn found herself the only one of five adults on the farm who did not succumb to measles so, in addition to all the daily chores, she had a ward of patients for several weeks. Then, over a holiday period when six children (plus her three) were at the station, a polio epidemic struck the country and no children were permitted to travel, so Evelyn had nine children to care for until the quarantine period was lifted.

There were house parties in those days too: Evelyn remembered wonderful dances at Irishman Creek, Rhoborough Downs and Simons Hill. No special accommodation was needed, as guests would bunk down in the shearers' quarters, in a spare bedroom, or even outside. After one particular party at Simons Hill, 40 people showed up for breakfast. Providing food for a party never bothered Evelyn. She found the secret was to offer a limited number of items, such as sandwiches, mince tarts and cream sponges, in large quantities.

A pipe band had been formed over at Irishman Creek, and the members of the band played for the guests at one of the Simons Hill house parties, which, for Evelyn, made the evening perfect. In the music room, 30 couples could easily dance at the same time. Seats were arranged around the room and the floors would be well dusted.

Evelyn made light of her many accomplishments. She somehow found the time to gift an organ to the Church of the Good Shepherd at Tekapo, and to play for the church services every week from the time the church opened in 1935 until her retirement in 1955. When her daughter married, she made the wedding dress, the bridesmaids' dresses and the food for the wedding reception. Her energy and capacity seemed to be unlimited.

Soon after their arrival at Simons Hill, Evelyn mentioned to a local agent, who was visiting the station in the first 12 months they were there, that they would probably get out when their five years were up. The agent nodded wisely and told her that she would find, after that time, that a team of horses would not move them. He was right. Evelyn and William grew to love their life at Simons Hill and remained there for 45 years, eventually retiring to Timaru when one of their sons took up the property. She lived

Looking out to the mountains from the new Simons Hill homestead. MARY HOBBS

to see him growing great paddocks of lucerne and clover on the same spot where she had lamented the bare ground and endless tussocks. There is now a water race running through the parched land where she stood all those years ago, and healthy lambs are regularly being sent off to the market.

Evelyn's daughter, also Evelyn, married an engineer, Donald Middlemiss, who was working at Irishman Creek Station and the couple spent many happy years bringing up their family there.

After Evelyn's son Ron took over Simons Hill, and he was later joined by his nephew, Peter. Ron, a passionate farmer, won many accolades for stock, wool and crops. Once Ron retired, however, Peter opted for a life-style change and the station was sold. After 83 years, Simons Hill passed from the Hosken family into new hands.

Around the time Simons Hill was put on the market, Denis Fastier and his partner, Jane Stevenson, had been searching for a station for about a year. They had sold their station in Queensberry, Otago, in 1993. When they left Central Otago they searched every gully between Glenorchy and the Marlborough Sounds, as well as Tasmania, in their quest for some land they could afford, in an area that really spoke to them.

The Mackenzie Country was not looking its best in the early 1990s, as the rabbit population had again escalated out of control, yet each district they considered had its own problems. The Wairau, too, had trouble with pests. On a night shoot they were getting the same number of possums and hares as the Mackenzie farmers were getting rabbits. The Wairau also had a weed and wasp problem. Over in the Waimate, wallabies were increasing in large numbers.

Jane had noticed several rabbits around Simons Hill when they looked over the property, but this land was the closest they had come to finding what they wanted, so they took the plunge. The station had been leased out by the Hoskens to another party and there was a caveat on the title, but Peter Hosken assured Denis and Jane that he would sort that out and urged them to move in and start farming. Jane and Denis arrived with their ute, their sheep and a tent. Luckily, the situation with the previous lease was resolved, as they had sold the stock remaining on Simons Hill when they arrived and replaced it with their own.

But the rabbit problem seemed to have reached plague-like proportions in the few months since they bought Simons Hill. This is no surprise considering, according to a clipping from a rural magazine Denis found, it is possible for one pair of rabbits to increase the population by nine million in only three years.[9] They began tackling the rabbits with night shooting, but the animals would disappear just out of the light, so the shoot was not as productive as hoped. Their winter assault was better as tracks in the snow led them to the burrows, where gas was inserted to kill the rabbits. Despite these efforts, they, like all the other farmers in the district, had to face the fact that they were fighting a losing battle. Pasture was being eaten out, trees and shrubs were hit and soil erosion was escalating, owing to the number of burrows and minimal cover remaining. It was a fast way to go broke.

In desperation the farmers collectively appealed to the government for permission for the rabbit haemorrhagic disease (RHD) virus to be released in order to deal with the problem but, in July 1997, the government refused. Some farmers brought the virus in illegally and distributed it. Controversial though RHD was, it had an instant effect. For the first time in years the farmers from South Canterbury to Otago had some breathing space. Some rabbits are now beginning to develop immunity to RHD and numbers are climbing, particularly in Otago, but on Simons Hill the numbers remain low, largely because the family constantly kept on top of the rabbits through night shooting. On some nights, Denis, Jane and Denis's son, Glenn, would cull around 225 rabbits on a shoot. They were out there in all weathers, sometimes with icicles hanging from their balaclavas.

Winters can be brutal to stock as well. It can get particularly cold here with the thermometer registering as low as -21°C on one occasion. In the snow of 1995, just a year after Denis and Jane arrived, even the water in the tread of the tractor tyres froze as they were feeding out. In those years, as soon as they had fed out they would gas the rabbit holes to keep the numbers down.

There was no let-up. It was eight years before they could find the time to get away for just two nights – to climb, on a perfect day, Nun's Veil near Mount Cook Station, with guide Nic Kagan. Their rare holidays were a break from the station, but they were always active ones. They also climbed the beautiful Minarets on the Main Divide from the West Coast side, Mount Hooker and Mount Barff, followed by Taranaki, Ngauruhoe and Ruapehu in the North Island.

Back at Simons Hill, their main challenge was to find ways in which the land could be made more productive. The couple looked at new crops they could grow and investigated their export potential. For several seasons they tried rosehips, as they grow well in the Mackenzie, and the fruit can sell for a substantial price. However, the project was not as profitable as first thought, so was later shelved.

With another couple, Denis and Jane invested in growing giant sunflowers for birdseed and many hectares graced the Mackenzie for a time. Denis noted that if 2 hectares were planted, birds would eat it all, but if 40 hectares were planted, the birds would still only take 2 hectares. The sunflowers grew well, they looked spectacular and there was high demand for the birdseed, but because they were on unirrigated land they were more subject to the vagaries of the weather. Other challenges included difficulties in removing the tough stalks after harvesting. A lot of machinery was broken in the process.

Denis was one of the farmer coordinators for a lupin-growing project in the high country. These plants were found to be more suited to a slightly higher rainfall than Simons Hill and to soil with higher acidity. Like all legumes, lupins fix nitrogen in the soil and boost production in the nitrogen-deficient Mackenzie. There are different schools of thought on lupins, but this perceived pest can be innovatively utilised for its good qualities, while reducing the need for expensive fertilisers, and providing good feed for sheep. (To keep the lupins under control, it is important to ensure the sheep graze on them at the right time.) Denis has perfected the art of achieving a high yield of legumes on the station. This was most recently acknowledged with a Grasslands Award for Innovation and Pasture Establishment, which he was eventually persuaded to accept on the proviso that it was awarded to all at Simons Hill.

Several years ago Denis and Jane moved out of the old homestead built by William Hosken and into a new home on the hill behind, which commands a spectacular view of Aoraki/Mt Cook and the surrounding mountains. The house, made of timber cut on the station, is heated with a furnace fuelled by wood. Solar power harnesses the sun's energy during the day, with the concrete floor soaking up the sun and emitting the heat at night. In winter, if there is no sun, the furnace does the same job with its underfloor water pipes heating the house. There is no need for any other heating. Generous plantings of the natives that thrive in this climate surround the house.

Denis grew up in Dunedin, although not on a farm, but the rural life seemed a natural fit when he was introduced to it in his twenties and he is very much at home at Simons Hill. Jane, who grew up in North Canterbury, has been on farms or high country stations all her life. She endured four years in the city when she went to high school in Christchurch, then explored the world before returning to muster in the high country with her beloved dogs. She has covered thousands of hectares of high country terrain on her beats on different stations in the South Island.

Jane and Denis make a great team and vast improvements have been made under their careful stewardship of Simons Hill. The station is in great shape, which is all down to excellent management and a tremendous amount of effort. Denis also invented an implement to pull slightly larger wilding pines out with his tractor. That and a lot of hard labour help keep them under control. Whether it is the odd rogue spread of a sycamore, or rams that need a cull – any detail of station life – they are both onto it. They see far and the future excites them.

Denis's son, Glenn, his wife Sarah and their three children, Fred, Stella and Baxter, live in the original homestead. Glenn works the station with his father and Jane, and they also employ another farm worker, Mark. Denis's daughter, Bron, is on Twin Peaks Station, south of Omarama, with her husband Mark Becker and their two sons, Cody and Ryan.

The old shearing shed. MARY HOBBS

Glenn's grandparents on his mother's side originally farmed Locharburn Station in Otago. His grandfather grew up on Lowburn Station and later purchased Locharburn and Ben Nevis. Glenn believes that it is not about how many generations farm a station, but about the amount of passion one has for farming, because that is what makes it work. Denis often sought advice from others who were experts in their field and Glenn, too, has found it beneficial to be in contact with these people and their knowledge.

Sarah grew up in Ashburton and her family moved onto a farm when she was 13. A good part of her life has always included music. As a mez-zo-soprano, she trained under some fine New Zealand teachers. Her early travels took her to Europe, but 10 years later she returned to Italy, where she was invited to join the Assisincanto Chorus. Although a great privilege, this was not paid work, so she lived frugally and supported herself working as an au pair to a family in Assisi, while studying Italian in Perugia each day. When she met Glenn in Christchurch she had just returned from Italy and was working in the blackcurrant industry. (Her parents have been growing blackcurrants in Canterbury for the last 30 years.)

Glenn had gained good experience by securing well-paid seasonal farm work in England, Scotland, the United States and Canada, and also travelled in Western Europe, the Middle East, Africa and Asia. He was not sure what he wanted to do when he left high school, but studied at Lincoln University anyway. It was not until he went overseas that he began to appreciate how lucky he was to be able to live on the land in New Zealand. In 2001, he returned to work at Simons Hill with his father.

The couple married in Ashburton at St Andrew's Presbyterian Church on 4 April 2009. On their wedding day, they discovered Glenn's great-grandparents had married in the same church many years before.

Glenn reckons it would have been great to farm in his grandfather's time when there was less paperwork and more physical activity. Compliance requirements today involve recording pretty much everything that is done on the farm, including stock movement, animal health records, health and safety, fertiliser applications, nutrient loss and water quality and irrigation monitoring, and information to pass standards for the sale of meat and wool. New plant, maintenance of older machinery, fencing and pest control all come at substantial expense.

Glenn feels that overgrazing can be substantially reduced if the hill country is well subdivided into smaller blocks. Although this requires an increase in stock movement, there is less risk of soil erosion and grazing keeps the weeds down.

One of the things Glenn loves most about farming is that, despite the difficulties, the success is visible, which provides reassurance that you are heading in the right direction. When the crops are good, when the lamb percentage steadily increases, when the wool clip is of the finest quality, and when the station is able to carry more stock on less land and not suffer for it – these are all things that can be seen. Glenn believes it is always important to celebrate the wins, even the small gains, not just lament the losses.

Glenn can take his daughter Stella out to move the hoggets with him, and he and Sarah enjoy the times when their young son Fred wanders out in the morning and says something like, 'Mount Cook is looking good today, Mum.' The two families have a genuine desire to improve the property and they work hard at it. They do not talk much about their love for the land, but you can see it on their faces, and feel it in the way they speak. It goes deep.

Denis and Jane with Sarah, Glenn and their children. Shepherd Mark Chapman is on the far right. MARY HOBBS

IRISHMAN CREEK

On the road from Christchurch to Queenstown, between Tekapo and Twizel, travellers pass a quaint blue and white mailbox, about the size of a small shed. Starlings nest in its eaves. In spring, it is surrounded by lupins of all shades. It was built in 1921 and has since acted as a landmark among the tussock-covered, rolling hills. Who has lived here? What historic stories does this land hold?

Irishman Creek, often affectionately known as Irishman, was named after a creek on the station thickly bordered with matagouri, which is also commonly known as 'wild Irishman'. At some stage there was also a human 'Wild Irishman', for there is an old story of two surveyors lost in a storm, long before the original homestead was built, who had heard of a hut near the creek. Desperate to get out of the wild weather, they finally arrived at the hut to find an Irishman with a rifle over his shoulder, marching up and down outside, shouting, 'Who goes there?' Apparently it took some time to disarm the chap so they could make their way inside without being shot.[1]

In 1921 Bill (later Sir William) Hamilton purchased Irishman Creek from Mrs Egerton Reid. In those days it was 9000 hectares of bare, rolling tussock country, with the great range of the Southern Alps visible in the distance. There was not a tree in sight. (Bill is said to have planted 1000 trees a year for half a century and his legacy now shelters the homestead and the lake he made close by.) Its boundaries on the west were Lake Pukaki, and the Tekapo River on the east, with Irishman Creek and Maryburn Stream meandering in between.

The iconic Irishman Creek mailbox in spring. MARY HOBBS

Bill, born in 1899, grew up on the 18,000-hectare Ashwick Station, near Fairlie, so was no stranger to life in the high country. In those days, you had to make what was needed or go without, and even as a child Billy had little difficulty in defining a problem and working out how to solve it. He was the personification of the innovative Kiwi 'can do' attitude. He was blessed with a mother who had read that children should be able to 'run wild' until they were seven, before settling down to any lessons. And run wild Billy and his two sisters, Leila and Kitty, did, learning so much from their outdoor classroom.

Billy loved going off to camp with local rabbiter Bill Shute and his pack of 23 dogs. They would often be in the back country for weeks on end. The first stop was usually Burkes Pass Hotel, where old Bill would get 'refreshments' while Billy waited outside, for what seemed like hours, taking care of the horse. Much later Shute would stagger out with more supplies and they would set off again, eventually stopping at a roadman's hut at Edwards Creek for lunch, which was usually cold chops with tea

made in a treacle tin. When they branched off the road, they loaded the gear onto the horse and tramped the rest of the journey to a musterer's hut. It was all an adventure to Billy. They lived on duck, rabbit and eel. As Bill's future wife Peggy wrote in her book, *Wild Irishman*, 'It was a real Huckleberry Finn life.'[2] Bill used to tell Peggy that he learned more from old Bill Shute than anyone.

Billy also took great pleasure in floating a homemade canoe down the river, but he found the tediousness of dragging it back up along the bank intolerable. 'Why not make a trailer for it? And why not a dog to pull the trailer?' He retrieved some wood, a couple of old bicycle tyres, some old harness, and, with a bit of help from one of the workman, made a trailer to carry the canoe and, with old straps and dog-collars, a harness for the dog. His big brown retriever was not 'madly keen' at first, but Bill trained him patiently until the dog became so proud of his job that he would allow no other dog to wear his harness. This was a great improvement, but Bill remained unsatisfied: he still had to take the canoe from the trailer and back to the launching site. 'If only there was such a thing as a boat which could make it upstream as well as down!'[3] And there on the river, in the South Canterbury high country on that day, the dream for the world-famous Hamilton jet boat was first conceived.

One day Billy, aged about eight, was invited to accompany Charlie Elms, a driver for Wigley & Jones Motors of Fairlie, to Mount Cook in his lorry. After leaving at 4 a.m. they had a bite to eat at Pukaki and finally arrived at the old Hermitage by 9 p.m. Billy was given accommodation in the driver's hut, which also happened to be occupied by Jock Richmond, a mountain guide, who kindly took Billy under his wing and introduced him to the other mountain guides, Peter and Alex Graham, Jack Lippe and Jack Clarke. Billy sat by the fire with them and listened in awe to their stories of mountains and the mountaineers who climbed them.

While still a boy, Billy made a sand yacht constructed from an old windmill and old bicycle wheels. Unfortunately it required drilling holes in angle iron by hand. When it was finished he sailed down the road between Ashwick and the neighbouring property, but soon became unpopular because he frightened the local horses.

In 1912, when Billy was just 13, he resolved to build a workshop, because he knew that if he wanted to avoid drilling holes by hand again he

would need power. He came up with the solution of a waterwheel, which he built. He then made a dam for the waterwheel by diverting water from a water-race into a gully. The next step was to create an open gravity-fed channel to carry the water from the dam to the waterwheel. By the time he had finished, he had a system that successfully drove a generator that created enough power to light Ashwick homestead and run a small lathe, as well as a drill and emery wheel. This was two years before the New Zealand government began operating its first hydro-electric station at Lake Coleridge. Billy's waterwheel and dam supplied electricity for the homestead until the 1930s when they were connected to the national grid.

In 1916, this happy family was struck the first of two severe blows, when Bill's beloved older half-brother and mentor, Cyril, was killed in action in Egypt early in August. Then, in May 1922, Bill's vivacious sister Leila Georgeson died in Timaru from septicaemia, 10 days after giving birth to her son, Sholto. Apparently the cause was the unwashed hands of the doctor.

ABOVE The 1914 Isle of Man Tourist Trophy Sunbeam at Muriwai Beach, Auckland, 1925. HAMILTON COLLECTION
OPPOSITE Bill Hamilton, an accomplished ice skater, tows his son, Jon, and daughter, June, on the family ice rink in about 1930. HAMILTON COLLECTION

The family were devastated by the deaths, and Bill's father was not well. In 1923, Bill's parents decided to take a break and visit their daughter Kitty and her husband, who were living in England, and asked young Bill to go with them. He was reluctant, as he had just purchased the 9000-hectare Irishman Creek Station and had a lot of work ahead of him. However, he did go on the trip and it changed his life.

While in England, Bill purchased a classic Isle of Man Sunbeam racing car and diligently put hours of work into it. Through mutual friends he also met his future wife, Peggy Wills, who had grown up on the family farms in Devon and Berkshire. Her father owned the shipping company, George Wills & Sons. Peggy had contributed to the war effort by working long hours, six days a week, in a munitions factory in England, years she later described in her book, *Three Years, or the Duration: The Memoirs of a Munition Worker 1914–1918*. Peggy also suffered tragedy when her beloved brother, Oliver, who was a pilot, was killed the day before Armistice Day. Peggy had visited New Zealand with her family in 1919 and even on her first visit found the country 'held a special attraction'.[4]

Peggy saw Bill's Sunbeam racing car outside her friend's house before she met its owner. She was warned not to go out in it, as it was built for the track and she would probably break her neck. Peggy immediately ignored the advice when Bill suggested a run. They visited each other regularly while Bill was in Britain – hiking over Dartmoor, and camping in Scotland with Peggy's brother Matthew – and on their return to London, Bill asked Peggy to marry him. The wedding took place in October 1923, after which they returned home to Irishman Creek.

Two years later Matthew Wills came out to New Zealand and subsequently purchased Opawa Station. His son, Gavin, was a mountain guide at Aoraki/Mount Cook, but for many years has run an internationally known gliding company based at Omarama. Peggy's sister, Lucy, came to New Zealand in 1926 and bought Tekapo Station in 1928, so Peggy was never far from her family.

For Peggy, in 1923, travelling through Burkes Pass and over into the Mackenzie Basin was 'like entering a new world', and it is the same today, as the traveller swoops up the last bend, and round the final corner of the long cutting, to see the breathtaking Mackenzie Country suddenly spread out below: 'The Mackenzie is never green like the country we have just left, but a velvety golden brown, surrounded by mountains, the Alps in the far distance always capped by snow.'[5]

Back then, the road was little more than a shingle track that Peggy initially found disconcerting. The constant noise of stones thumping beneath the car made talking a challenge, but it didn't stop Bill giving Peggy the history behind the landmarks they passed. Dog Kennel Corner, he told her, was named at the point between Rollesby and Sawdon stations, where the road cut through a fence that divided them. A dog was placed there so that its barking would keep the sheep from the two properties apart. Dead Man's Creek was named after a shepherd who died of exposure in the 1800s. His faithful dog was found beside him with four dead weka he had laid closely to his boss's body, so he would have food when he woke. Whisky Cutting recalled the sad day when a shearer's wagon overturned and all the jars of whisky on board crashed into the ditch.

Then Peggy arrived at Irishman Creek. The house was small, primer pink in colour and topped by an unpainted corrugated iron roof, with rambling roses climbing up the side and over the porch. The kitchen contained an old coal range and the kettle was constantly on the boil for cups of tea. Peggy was introduced to the housekeeper, who had charge of Bill's nephew, Dick Georgeson (whose mother was Leila), another nephew of her own and the garden. There were also introductions to Bill's horses and dogs. On this hot nor'wester day, the lure of Irishman Creek proved too much for Peggy and she succumbed to the urge for a swim in the crystal-clear mountain water. As she and Bill relaxed and looked across to the mountain range in the distance, he introduced her to each of the peaks. 'I did not mind the bareness and the isolation,' Peggy remembered. 'I loved the feel of it.'[6]

In today's high-powered world of communication devices, Peggy's introduction to her new home and the subsequent swim sound idyllic, but there are always challenges living in such an environment, even in the twenty-first century. Chief among these is the weather and, to a certain extent, the isolation, though that is also part of the attraction. In those days supplies arrived only once a year by traction engine, carrying flour, salt, oatmeal, sugar, and chests of tea. On its return journey it was loaded with wool for sale.

The usual fare was lamb chops for breakfast, mutton for lunch and

tea, 'until winter when a bullock was shot and hung frozen in the trees; then we lived on beef until it was finished'.[7] Peggy supplemented their diet with ducks, fowls and turkeys reared at Irishman. Milk and butter were made on the station, along with bread and soap. All the meat had to be prepared from live animals – slaughtered, cut into sections, or plucked, gutted and roasted, fried or boiled. Peggy confessed to Bill she was not talented in the culinary arts, but he did not care: he wanted his wife to help him with the sheep, which she was more than happy to do.

Regardless of Peggy's lack of talent in the kitchen, it remained a room that was the focus of family and farm life. It was where Peggy greeted swaggers who used to roam the district in the 1920s; on one particular day 15 turned up searching for a bed and food for the night.

Annie Carter, an old friend of Peggy's family, whom she adored, had come out from England with Matthew Wills and she took care of the housework and gardening, as Peggy was most often helping Bill on the station.

The original house has been moved and extended, but the old coal range still stands there. It's the same one that Peggy and Annie warmed their feet in when it was so cold one winter that bottles burst, foodstuffs

164

froze, steam from the kettle froze on the ceiling and spilt water on the stairs became an icy puddle within minutes.

In 1925 Peggy, who was expecting her first child, waited for the results of the New Zealand Motor Cup, which Bill had entered and which was held on the beach at Muriwai. Two chaps heard the outcome at Fairlie and dropped in with the happy news that Bill won the cup and had broken the Australasian speed record with official speeds of 160 kilometres per hour. Peggy, still in bed when they arrived, 'felt like Victoria being woken from her sleep to be told she was Queen'.[8]

Bill entered in many races and enjoyed great success, including another Australasian record achieved in Invercargill in 1928, where he was clocked at 175.5 kph. In 1930 he entered his Bentley in three races at the Brooklands Easter Meeting in England, and won them all – the first driver to achieve this feat. Peggy almost always accompanied Bill to his races and many of their adventures on these circuits are relayed in her book.

A workshop was built at Irishman Creek in the 1920s. There were no council bylaws or building code compliances, so Bill could just drive to Ashwick Station, cut down the trees required for the construction, transport them and construct the workshop. But he needed power, for his home and his workshop, and he had the perfect place for a hydro plant: a terrace above an empty cottage. Bill decided to redesign his family's house and attach it to the cottage. 'In no time the house was cut in half. One piece was left and the other put up on skids and pulled through the two streams of the creek by traction engine and planted beside the cottage to be joined together'.[9] While these alterations were taking place, Bill and Peggy shared a draughty garage with four-month-old June, the nanny shared a tent with their young son Jon, four-year-old Dick was in another tent, and the man who worked for them in yet another.

They eventually moved back into the newly completed house in May 1927 and had the luxury of blazing electric light after dealing with lamps and candles. Their joy was short-lived, however, as they were about to experience one of the coldest winters in the Mackenzie. First there was a dimming of lights. They found ice clogging the turbine, so Bill and Peggy spent a morning 'clawing this ice out with our hands'. Then the

water pipes in the house burst, causing a flood inside. Buckets were put out, candles were lit and everyone huddled around the old range in the kitchen or the fireplace in the bedroom for warmth. Bottles burst because of their expanding frozen contents, and bread and milk had to be thawed out every morning. Even the water race carrying the water for the hydro scheme froze. The men tried to break up the ice in the creek and when one chap grabbed a crowbar with his bare hands, he became stuck to it.

Bill's final solution was to build a dam so he could take the water for the hydro plant from beneath the ice. The only scoops available to dig out the dam were ancient: according to Bill, it was like trying to dig the dirt out with a salt-spoon. Ever inventive, he designed a new scoop, which attracted a lot of interest, nationally and internationally.

Bill was able to procure steady contracting jobs for earth-moving scoops and other equipment during the Depression, when the price of wool was so low it was barely worth growing. Carving out the airstrip at Pukaki was one of the first jobs with the scoop. Many others followed, including the first airstrip at Mount Cook.

Peggy's father was very interested in the scoop, so the family went back to England again in 1936, where Bill made another scoop for a company interested in selling it over there. While away, Peggy was shocked to hear about the German animosity towards Jewish people. When she returned to New Zealand, she vigorously lobbied the government to allow some Jews to immigrate. As a result, Dr Helmut Pappe and his wife Vera came to New Zealand in 1939 and moved to Irishman Creek. Dr Pappe, who had been part of the Faculty of Law and Economics in Wrocław, Poland, later played a large part in the building of Bill's company. The Pappes spoke five languages and taught Jon, June and Dick German, French and Latin. They were also given classes in Shakespeare, in addition to lessons from the Correspondence School.[10]

In the early days, when the lagoons froze over, the family and those who worked on the station began ice skating. Peggy tucked baby son Jon in blankets and left him to sleep among the tussocks while they slid around, with or without skates. They also invented a rudimentary hockey game, with gumboots serving as goalposts and tree branches as hockey sticks. They would bounce back home on the truck, often bruised and sore, and sit around the fire laughing together about their day. In later

The engineering workshop at Irishman Creek. HAMILTON COLLECTION years, Peggy recalled 'how good they were, those days together out in the crisp Mackenzie winter; snow all around us, the long line of Alps shining white in the distance, and over all a clear, still sky'.[11]

When Peggy's parents treated them to a trip back to England in earlier years, they watched professional skaters at several shows, amazed at their grace and elegance. Bill made a small ice rink on the station when they returned. Unfortunately the ice surface was rough and the conventional options for making it smoother were inadequate, so Bill turned his hand to inventing a way to keep it maintained so it would remain smooth. Another machine was created that scraped the snow from the ice with little effort.

Friends came from all over the place to join in the fun. There was a fancy dress party held on the ice, and even a play. The Irishman Creek ice hockey team remained the unbeaten winners of the district for many years, competing at Mount Cook, Tekapo, Albury and Mount Harper. By the lovely Blue Lake, where William Spotswood Green and his party had camped in the 1800s on their way to Mount Cook, and where the Guinness family of Glentanner and others used to picnic, the Irishman Creek players battled it out on the ice against the Hermitage team. A well-known local painter, Duncan Darroch, donned a kilt and piped the opposing teams onto the rink. Although the teams became very adept, it was never serious; they simply played for the joy of it. And Bill was the lively spirit behind it all, his enthusiasm and drive so infectious that everyone gladly followed in his wake.

Other impromptu social events arose in more whimsical fashion. On a cold, dark night in winter, the women on the station felt that it was all getting a bit dreary, so Peggy decided they should put on every piece of jewellery they owned with their best dresses and all their finery, and wear it to dinner. It was an outstanding success. They were in the middle of this outrageous event when there was a loud knock at the door. Peggy answered it, weighed down with jewellery. It was a bus driver on his way to the Hermitage with 24 guests. The weather was bad and the bus had broken down. Could they take shelter? Peggy gaily waved them all in and made them welcome.

Other inventions that Bill created in his workshop included a water sprinkler for the vegetables, which moved up and down the garden, a lift

for stacking hay, an air compressor for the forge in the workshop and an air-conditioning plant for June's room, to help with her hay fever. Another later invention, which Bill considered his best, was the loader-dozer. It was a tractor with a blade at the front that enabled the driver to scoop up a load, raise it above his head and dump its contents on the other side into an open truck, without any need for turning or swivelling. This meant much less wear and tear on the vehicles.

Bill was creating earth-moving equipment for the International Harvester Company when war broke out in 1939. As the threat from Japan came closer, there was an urgent call in New Zealand for the manufacture of munitions. Bill and his team at Irishman Creek manufactured them for the remainder of the war. For Peggy it must have felt like déjà vu. So now, as well as the production of earth-moving machines, the station was churning out 'parts for Bren gun carriers, rifles, machine-gun and trench mortars'. Some of this needed 'great precision and working to fine tolerances', which all added to the pressure.[12] Bill was also asked to make safety catches for rifles, as no one else the government had approached had been willing to do it.

One of Bill's most outstanding attributes was his ability to teach unskilled people to do high-precision work. He also made the workshop available to them for their own personal use. At the height of production, more than 40 engineers were working at Irishman, and only four of them had any previous experience. Most of them had been rabbiters, station hands or musterers. There was also a salesperson, a caretaker and even a hairdresser.

Some great people found their way to the station. Among them were Don Middlemiss, who had done contract work for Bill before the war, and Evelyn Hosken from Simons Hill (not to be confused with her mother of the same name). The couple became engaged before Don went off to war and after he returned in 1943 they married at Irishman Creek, piped in by the station band. They worked together as engineers in the workshop and lived in a small home on the property, where their daughter Raewyn

Some of the stars of the Irishman Creek workshop, from left, Dick Georgeson, Roy Rappley, Dave Small, Janet Richards, Bill McNeary, Bill Geeves, Bill Bain, Helmut Pappe, Stewart Fraser, Frank Atkinson, Alf Hosken, Jon Hamilton. HAMILTON COLLECTION

grew up. Life was made easier for employees with children, as a school was constructed at Irishman Creek and a school bus collected other children from the area and delivered them to the station for lessons.

Evelyn, now almost 100, still fondly remembers the 20 years she spent at Irishman Creek. She loved every moment of it and spoke highly of Peggy and Bill and their wonderful hospitality, which made her and Don feel part of their extended family. All employees were invited to the big house if someone came to play music, so everyone could enjoy it. There was also an annual Christmas party that Peggy and Bill held in their home for the staff. Evelyn and Don later moved to Christchurch and worked for Bill's company there.

Evelyn's brother, Alf Hosken, also came to help during the war years. Particularly skilled at training the staff, he later took over the management of the workshop at the station. Fire was a great risk in the workshop, so a hydrant was designed and built, and fire drills were held every Friday. For every potential problem or challenge, Bill had a workable solution. The first hydraulic pumps were also designed and built at Irishman Creek. The use of hydraulics eliminated the need for gears, clutches or inching motors, so the operator could work the machine with one lever.[13] The company became pioneers in this field.

After the war, faced with an increased requirement for the agricultural and earthmoving equipment they were manufacturing, Bill had the choice of remaining at Irishman, with its limitations of distance, or moving to a main centre to expand his engineering firm. Bill chose the latter, but still retained ownership of his beloved Irishman Creek, where he was free to concentrate, with his son Jon, and other valued employees such as engineer George Davison, on the design and manufacture of what was to become the world-famous Hamilton Jet. Jon and George made further advances to the original design, which all culminated in the superior product now available worldwide. Jon's son, Mike Hamilton, later designed larger jets that enabled them to be utilised for deep-water use overseas.

Immediately after the war, in 1945, Bill's new factory was built on a 4-hectare site at Middleton, Christchurch. Under his direction, the company developed loader-dozers, road graders, loaders, mobile cranes, ditch-diggers, front-end hydraulic loaders, mobile cranes, excavators, bridges, railway wagons and massive control gates for hydro-power stations, as well as the huge penstock lines for the power stations in the Mackenzie and Waitaki regions. Bill also created the first ski tow, which was erected on Coronet Peak in 1947, and then the tow for Ruapehu.[14] This factory went on to produce bridge girders and rail wagons. The company also constructed the 120-metre Kawarau Bridge near Queenstown, which was made in sections and transported to the site. The precision was so exact that, when all of the sections were joined together, there was just a 3-millimetre gap. Then, in 1954, trials of the first jet boat began.

Even when the company in Christchurch grew to about 500 employees, in the 1980s, the tradition of looking after the staff continued. The benefits included a subsidised cafeteria, superannuation, a social club, an annual ball, a swimming pool and playing fields.

Leila's son Dick Georgeson, whom Peggy and Bill brought up as their own, worked for Bill for many years and became general manager in 1972. In *The Leading Edge*, written with his wife, Anna Wilson, Dick describes their great pride in discovering that, in New York on 9/11, ferryboats powered by Hamilton Jets shifted more people out of Manhattan that day than any other craft.[15] The jet units are also used worldwide by coastline police, tourism companies and oil rig companies. Bill and Peggy's grandson, Michael Hamilton, is currently in charge of the company, with Keith Whiteley as the managing director.

Dick had always harboured a dream to fly. A visit to England in the late 1940s introduced him to gliding, which became a lifelong passion. By 1960, Dick was the holder of a world record in gliding and by 1979 he was awarded the most prestigious award given by the Fédération Aéronautique Internationale (FAI) – the World Air Sports Federation. In 1985 he was the recipient of the Lilienthal Medal, the highest award for gliding and in 1979 he received an MBE for Services to Aviation in New Zealand. Bill was often out there giving Dick a tow to get him airborne, swearing that he was sure he was airborne in the truck before Dick was airborne in the glider.

The jet boat was Bill's most famous product. He was initially keen to develop it so he and Peggy could enjoy more camping, fishing and picnics on the surrounding rivers and lakes. Bill always acknowledged Archimedes as the true inventor, but he took it further, and, with a close team of engineers, designed a jet boat that would propel at very high speed with the advantage of a shallow draught. The majority of the test work was carried out in the many rivers of the high country, and on the dam behind the homestead at Irishman.

ABOVE American scientist, Bill Austin took this photo of Bill in 1958 at Broken River, a tributary of the Waimakariri River. BILL AUSTIN
OPPOSITE Bill at his drawing board, Irishman Creek. HAMILTON COLLECTION

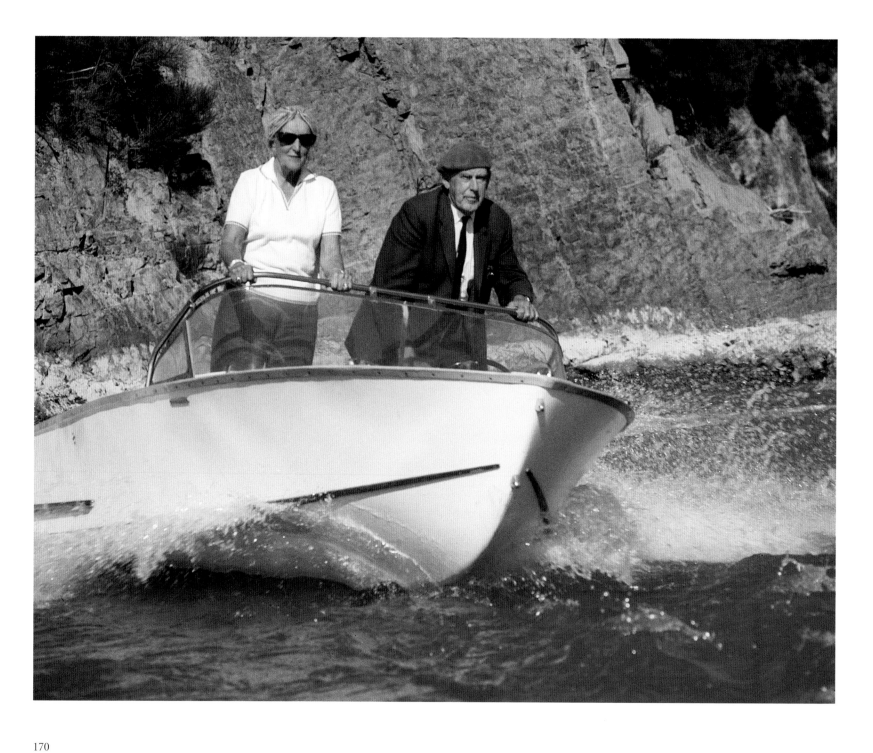

In 1959 Bill and Peggy travelled to the United States and made a reconnaissance trip by jet boat up the first 160 kilometres of the Colorado River into the lower reaches of the Grand Canyon. They intended to run upstream through the full length of the Grand Canyon the following year, but Bill fractured his arm while jet-boating in New Zealand, so his son Jon made the return trip to the Colorado River on Bill's behalf and drove the jet boat 740 kilometres down and then back up the famous river, which included Larva Falls, the most dangerous rapid on the Colorado.[16] In 1977 Jon and his son Michael joined Sir Edmund Hillary and some of his close friends on a great adventure up the Ganges River, from which, Sir Ed said, no one really returned the same.

Bill was very sad to see the changes in the Mackenzie Country landscape created by the hydro work. He realised it was unavoidable, and his company was involved with the engineering for it, but he knew and loved the rivers and lakes in this area so well and regretted that they had to be altered. He strongly supported open access to the waterways and their preservation.

In 1961, Bill was awarded a well-deserved OBE for 'very valuable service in the field of engineering and especially in the design and construction of the jet-propelled motorboat'. He was knighted in 1974. Four years later, when he died at Irishman, Peggy had a special rock split in half that she had dragged in from the station in the 1920s. This is the headstone that marks Bill's grave in Burkes Pass Cemetery, situated at the gateway to the high country they both loved. Peggy died at Irishman in 1982. The other half of the rock marks Peggy's grave, beside her beloved 'Wild Irishman', Bill.

In *The Leading Edge*, Dick describes Peggy as a remarkable and endearing woman who had room for him in addition to her own two children. She was always tolerant and loving, and gave him a great sense of security.[17] He credits her with first telling him about gliding, and with showing him what richness could be made from ordinary lives.

For some years, Peggy and Bill's daughter and son-in-law, June and Mick Morgan, were the next managing owners of Irishman Creek. Eventually they retired to Wanaka and their son, David, and his wife Sue, took over the management and ran a tourist operation from the station. The Hamilton Jet Museum was set up so visitors were able to tour through Bill's old workshop, then enjoy lunch in the family kitchen and dining room afterwards. David's brother, Mark, was also involved in running the station for a time.

In the late 1980s, by coincidence, glider pilots Justin Wills, a second cousin of Peggy's, and his wife Gillian were in New Zealand for a final visit before taking ownership of a new house in England. While they were over here, they received news that the sale had fallen through. They were en route back to England, when they received a call from David and Sue, who explained that Irishman might soon be up for sale. In 1989 Gillian and Justin became the proud owners of the station, and so Irishman Creek remained in the family.

One of Justin and Gillian's greatest joys at Irishman Creek has been developing an abiding love and admiration for merino sheep.

Justin's father, Phillip Wills, was a loved cousin of Peggy's and had been a pioneer of British gliding in the 1930s. He became world champion in 1952. Justin, too, has a formidable record in the sport. He was the National Champion of British Gliding several times, and won championships in the United States, Canada, Switzerland, France, Italy, Austria, Norway, South Africa and Japan. He was vice-world champion twice, thus making him one of the best glider pilots in the world.

Gillian also became a solo glider pilot and instructor and won a competition for the best beginner in her year, for which the prize was a glider. She was working for the British Gliding Association when she met Justin, appropriately, on an airfield. The couple married at Mount Cook in 1980, during one of their regular visits to New Zealand.

Reflecting on the history of Irishman Creek, Justin feels that the station became a social centre for people who did enterprising things, simply because of Bill. It was a place where things happened. Bill's special gift was the way in which he treated everyone, including the young, with enormous respect. You always felt that Bill was keen to help, he always understood where you were coming from, and he was always on your side. Peggy, too, was extremely special to Justin. He always thought that Peggy and Bill were a couple whose combined worth was so much more than just two people adding up to a team. It took both of them working together to create all that they did from Irishman Creek, each immensely encouraging of the other.

Whenever Bill Hamilton was reminded of his great triumphs, he used to say, 'Well, I had such a grand team of chaps with me.'[18] That comment is not surprising, for Bill created within people, a strong belief in themselves and a pride in their work, as well as a warm and friendly atmosphere to work in.

The next time you drive past the blue and white mailbox of Irishman Creek, think of all the great New Zealand history it symbolises. And tell your children that this was the home of legendary New Zealanders, who have proved, and continue to prove, that, with a dream, persistence, encouragement and enthusiasm, anything is possible.

OPPOSITE The drive into Irishman Creek. MARY HOBBS
OVERLEAF High country near Irishman Creek. MARY HOBBS

ENDNOTES

The Mary Range

1. Nicholas Chevalier (1828–1902) visited New Zealand three times and created some magnificent works of art, including *Lake Pukaki and Mount Cook in 1872 in the Evening*.
2. Unless otherwise noted, all material cited in this chapter comes from McHutcheson, William, 'The New Zealander at Home: Fifty years of colonial life; or, The Story of a Jubilee Colonist', *Otago Witness*, which appeared from 14 August to 30 October 1890 in 12 weekly episodes: 14 August, p. 34; 21 August, p. 32; 28 August, p. 36; 4 September, p. 36; 11 September, p. 36; 18 September, p. 36; 25 September, p. 36; 2 October, p. 31; 9 October, p. 31; 16 October, p. 30; 23 October, p. 30; and 30 October, p. 32.
3. Gordon Ogilvie, *Banks Peninsula: Cradle of Canterbury*, 3rd edn, Phillips & King, Christchurch, 2007, p. 85.
4. Ibid.
5. Robert Pinney, *Early South Canterbury Runs*, A.H. & A.W. Reed, Wellington, 1971, p. 161.

Birch Hill

1. William Vance, *High Endeavour: The Story of the Mackenzie Country*, first published by the author 1965, rev. edn, Reed, Wellington, 1980, p. 120.
2. Ibid., p. 54.
3. Ibid., p. 87.
4. *Timaru Herald*, 31 July 1888, p. 3.
5. Vance, *High Endeavour*, p. 144.
6. Johannes C. Andersen, *Jubilee History of South Canterbury*, Whitcombe & Tombs, Auckland, 1916, p. 463.
7. *Timaru Herald*, 3 February 1873, p. 3.
8. Ibid.
9. Andersen, *Jubilee History*, pp. 668, 756.

10. *Timaru Herald*, 3 February 1873, p. 3.
11. Andersen, *Jubilee History*, p. 463.
12. Mary Hobbs, *The Spirit of Mountaineering, Vol. 1. The Jack Adamson Story*, Spirit Ltd, Christchurch, 2007, p. 104.
13. Robert Pinney, *Early South Canterbury Runs*, A.H. & A.W. Reed, Wellington, 1971, p. 170.
14. *Timaru Herald*, 31 July 1888, p. 3.
15. Pinney, *Early South Canterbury Runs*, p. 170.

Mount Cook Station

1. William Vance, *High Endeavour: The Story of the Mackenzie Country*, first published by the author 1965, rev. edn, Reed, Wellington, 1980, p. 153.
2. Ibid., p. 38.
3. Johannes C. Andersen, *Jubilee History of South Canterbury*, Whitcombe & Tombs, Auckland, 1916, p. 457.
4. Vance, *High Endeavour*, pp. 152–153.
5. *Timaru Herald*, 3 February 1873, p. 3.
6. Vance, *High Endeavour*, p. 79.
7. William Spotswood Green, *The High Alps of New Zealand, Or, A Trip to the Glaciers of the Antipodes, With An Ascent of Mount Cook*, Macmillan, London, 1883, pp. 130, 132.
8. Vance, *High Endeavour*, p. 168.
9. *Evening Post*, 20 October 1928, p. 11.
10. *Evening Post*, 8 October 1930, p. 8.
11. Ibid., p. 19.
12. O.A. Gillespie, *South Canterbury: A Record of Settlement*, South Canterbury Centennial Committee, Timaru, 1958, p. 342.
13. Vance, *High Endeavour*, p. 89.
14. 'T.D. Burnett (1877–1941) – Man from the misty gorges', www.rootsweb.ancestry.com/~nzlscant/Burnett.htm

15. Ibid., p. 172.
16. Ibid., p. 154.
17. Ibid.
18. *Evening Post*, 20 October 1928, p. 11.
19. A site by Olwyn Whitehouse, www.rootsweb.ancestry.com, gives excellent details on the church, as does William Vance's *High Endeavour*.
20. *Timaru Herald*, 19 July 2010, www.rootsweb.ancestry.com/~nzls-cant/cavechurches.htm
21. Richard St Barbe Baker, *My Life, My Trees*, Findhorn, Forres, 1981, p. 137.
22. Janine Sundberg, interview with Catriona Baker, for 'A conversation with Catriona Baker', International Tree Foundation, UK, 2014.
23. Ibid.

Braemar

1. *Otago Witness*, 4 September 1890, p. 36.
2. *Press*, 5 March 1898, p. 7.
3. Ibid.
4. William Vance, *High Endeavour: The Story of the Mackenzie Country*, first published by the author 1965, rev. edn, Reed, Wellington, 1980, p. 159.
5. Matt Philp, *Heart of the Mackenzie: The Glenmore Station Story*, Random House, Auckland, 2014, p. 28.
6. Vance, *High Endeavour*, pp. 143, 149, 171, 211.
7. William Spotswood Green, *The High Alps of New Zealand, Or, A Trip to the Glaciers of the Antipodes, With An Ascent of Mount Cook*, Macmillan, London, 1883, p. 281.
8. Diana Rhodes, *With My Camera for Company, Havelock Williams 1884–1968: Adventures & Images of A Pioneering New Zealand Photographer*, Hazard Press, Christchurch, 2003, p. 150.
9. Philp, *Heart of the Mackenzie*, p. 34.
10. *Timaru Herald*, 12 August 1918, p. 9.
11. *Timaru Herald*, 1 February 1919, p. 11.
12. *Press*, 16 September 1925, p. 2.
13. *Evening Post*, 12 February 1930, p. 15.

Tasman Downs

1. Bruce Hayman, *The Nut that Changed My Life*, G.H., Wellington, 2007, p. 33.
2. Ibid., pp. 11–12.
3. Ibid., p. 73.
4. Ibid., p. 83.
5. Ibid., p. 87.
6. Ibid., p. 206.
7. Ibid., p. 215.
8. Ibid., p. 217.
9. Ibid., p. 222.
10. Ibid., p. 227.

The Wolds

1. William Vance, *High Endeavour: The Story of the Mackenzie Country*, first published by the author 1965, rev. edn, Reed, Wellington, 1980, p. 168.
2. 'The Squatters' Club', *Hocken Bulletin* No. 58, p. 2; also Timaru Herald, 10 September 1917, p. 2.
3. *Otago Witness 17 March 1898*; 'Squatters' Club'; Robert Pinney, *Early South Canterbury Runs*, A.H. & A.W. Reed, Wellington, 1971, p. 293.
4. Vance, *High Endeavour*, p. 168.
5. Ibid.
6. *Timaru Herald*, 10 September 1917, p. 2.
7. Noel Crawford. 'Grant, William', from the *Dictionary of New Zealand Biography. Te Ara – the Encyclopedia of New Zealand*, updated 2 October 2013, www.TeAra.govt.nz/en/biographies/2g17/grant-william
8. Vance, *High Endeavour*, p. 90.
9. *Timaru Herald*, 10 September 1917, p. 2.

Glentanner

1. William Vance, *High Endeavour: The Story of the Mackenzie Country*, first published by the author 1965, rev. edn, Reed, Wellington, 1980, p. 146.

2. 'Mackenzie Country, N.Z.', www.rootsweb.ancestry.com/~nzlscant/runs.htm#Glentanner
3. 'Early Mackenzie Country Graves – musterers', www.rootsweb.ancestry.com
4. Vance, *High Endeavour*, p. 102.
5. *Press*, 14 December 1885, p. 3.
6. Mary Hobbs, *The Spirit of Mountaineering, Vol. 1. The Jack Adamson Story*, Spirit Ltd, Christchurch, 2007, p. 104.
7. Vance, *High Endeavour*, p. 147.
8. *Timaru Herald*, 26 December 1895, p. 2.
9. L.G.D. Acland, *The Early Canterbury Runs*, 4th rev. edn, Whitcoulls, Christchurch, 1975, p. 229.
10. Ibid.
11. Ibid.
12. Vance, *High Endeavour*, p. 150.
13. *Dominion*, 27 February 1914, p. 8.
14. Vance, *High Endeavour*, p. 151.

Ferintosh

1. William Vance, *High Endeavour: The Story of the Mackenzie Country*, first published by the author 1965, rev. edn, Reed, Wellington, 1980, p. 152.
2. Betty Dick, *High Country Family*, A.H. & A.W Reed, Wellington, 1964, p. 25.
3. Dave Hansford, 'Wilding Pines', *New Zealand Geographic*, Issue 102, March–April 2010.

Ben Ohau

1. Brian Barry, Christchurch, 2001. Poem passed on by Brain Barry to Simon and Priscilla Cameron and kindly provided for this chapter.
2. Robert Pinney, *Early South Canterbury Runs*, A.H. & A.W. Reed, Wellington, 1971, pp. 53–54. Also William Vance, *High Endeavour: The Story of the Mackenzie Country*, first published by the author 1965, rev. edn, Reed, Wellington, 1980, pp. 138–139.
3. Ibid.
4. Ibid.

5. Helen Wilson, *My First Eighty Years*, Paul's Book Arcade, Hamilton, 1950, pp. 12–13.
6. Ibid.
7. Wilson, *My First Eighty Years*, p. 26.
8. Jane Honour Stronach memoirs, passed on by her descendants to Simon and Priscilla Cameron and kindly provided for this chapter.
9. Wilson, *My First Eighty Years*, pp. 13–14.
10. Ibid., p. 15.
11. Ibid., pp. 18–19.
12. Ibid., p. 20.
13. Ibid., p. 11.
14. Ibid., p. 20.
15. Jim McAloon. 'Land ownership – Centralisation after 1870', *Te Ara – the Encyclopedia of New Zealand*, updated 13 July 2012, www.TeAra.govt.nz/en/land-ownership/page-4
16. Wilson, *My First Eighty Years*, p. 22.
17. *Press*, 17 May 1879, p. 2.
18. *Timaru Herald*, 14 May 1879, p. 2.
19. Vance, *High Endeavour*, p. 140.
20. *North Otago Times*, 24 September 1879, p. 3.
21. All the following material, Jane Honour Stronach memoirs.
22. Robert Peden. 'Rabbits – Rabbits' impact on farming', *Te Ara – the Encyclopedia of New Zealand*, updated 13 July 2012 , www.TeAra.govt.nz/en/rabbits/page-2
23. Ibid.
24. Lynley Eade, *Twizel Town and Around: Remembering the Dam Days*, L.A. Irving, 2012, pp. 24, 25.
25. Ibid., p. 26.
26. Ibid., pp. 23–25.

Simons Hill

1. Evelyn Hosken, *Life on a Five Pound Note*, The Author, Timaru, 1964, p. 25.
2. Ibid.
3. Ibid., p. 26.
4. Ibid., p. 28.

5.   Ibid.

6.   Ibid., p. 31.

7.   Ibid., p. 61.

8.   Ibid., p. 63.

9.   This calculation, and how it was arrived at, was written in an article that Denis owns. It is dated 9 September 1990 and is entitled 'Rabbits' Habits'. Unfortunately, the name of the magazine could not be found.

Irishman Creek

1.   Peggy Hamilton, *Wild Irishman: The Story of Bill Hamilton, New Zealand Farmer, Inventor, Engineer, and Jet Boat Pioneer*, A.H. & A. W. Reed, Wellington, 1969, p. 96.

2.   Ibid., p. 30.

3.   Ibid., p. 17.

4.   Ibid., p. 85.

5.   Ibid., p. 92.

6.   Ibid., p. 94.

7.   Ibid., p. 112.

8.   Ibid., p. 123.

9.   Ibid., p. 130.

10. John Walsh, *Hamilton's Jet: The Biography of an Icon*, C.W.F. Hamilton & Co. Ltd, Christchurch, 2014, p. 27.

11. Hamilton, *Wild Irishman*, p. 142.

12. Ibid., p. 147.

13. Information from the old museum on the property, relayed with the kind permission of the current owners, Gillian and Justin Wills.

14. Walsh, *Hamilton's Jet*, pp. 97–99; also Hamilton, *Wild Irishman*, p. 161.

15. Dick Georgeson and Anna Wilson, *The Leading Edge: A Life in Gliding*, Georgeson Wilson, rev. edn., 2006.

16. Jon's wife Joyce wrote a book on their adventures, *White Water: The Colorado Jet Boat Expedition*, Caxton Press, Christchurch, 1963.

17. Georgeson and Wilson, *The Leading Edge*, p. 181.

18. Hamilton, *Wild Irishman*, p. 208.

BIBLIOGRAPHY

Newspapers

The following historic newspapers were accessed through Papers Past, the National Library of New Zealand's excellent online resource of digitised newspapers and periodicals: www.paperspast.natlib.govt.nz

Evening Post

Otago Witness, particularly McHutcheson, William, 'The New Zealander at Home: Fifty years of colonial life; or, The Story of a Jubilee Colonist', which appeared from 14 August to 30 October 1890 in 12 weekly episodes.

Press

Timaru Herald

Books

Acland, L.G.D., *The Early Canterbury Runs*, 4th rev. edn, Whitcoulls, Christchurch, 1975.

Andersen, Johannes, C., *Jubilee History of South Canterbury*, Whitcombe & Tombs, Auckland, 1916.

Dick, Betty, *High Country Family*, A.H. & A.W Reed, Wellington, 1964.

Eade, Lynley, *Twizel Town and Around: Remembering the Dam Days*, L.A. Irving, 2012.

Georgeson, Dick and Anna Wilson, *The Leading Edge: A Life in Gliding*, Georgeson Wilson, rev. edn., 2006.

Gillespie, O.A., *South Canterbury: A Record of Settlement*, South Canterbury Centennial Committee, Timaru, 1958.

Green, William Spotswood, *The High Alps of New Zealand, Or, A Trip to the Glaciers of the Antipodes, With An Ascent of Mount Cook*, Macmillan, London, 1883.

Hamilton, Peggy, *Wild Irishman: The Story of Bill Hamilton, New Zealand Farmer, Inventor, Engineer, and Jet Boat Pioneer*, A.H. & A. W. Reed, Wellington, 1969.

Hayman, Bruce, *The Nut that Changed My Life*, G.H., Wellington, 2007.

Hobbs, Mary, *The Spirit of Mountaineering, Vol. 1. The Jack Adamson Story*, Spirit Ltd, Christchurch, 2007.

Hosken, Evelyn, *Life on a Five Pound Note*, The Author, Timaru, 1964

Hosken, Evelyn, *Turn Back the Clock*, Reed, Wellington, 1968.

Philp, Matt, *Heart of the Mackenzie: The Glenmore Station Story*, Random House, Auckland, 2014.

Pinney, Robert, *Early South Canterbury Runs*, A.H. & A.W. Reed, Wellington, 1971.

Rhodes, Diana, *With My Camera for Company, Havelock Williams 1884–1968: Adventures & Images of A Pioneering New Zealand Photographer*, Hazard Press, Christchurch, 2003.

St Barbe Baker, Richard, *My Life, My Trees*, Findhorn, Forres, 1981.

Vance, William, *High Endeavour: The Story of the Mackenzie Country*, first published by the author 1965, rev. edn, Reed, Wellington, 1980.

Walsh, John, *Hamilton's Jet: The Biography of an Icon*, C.W.F. Hamilton & Co. Ltd, Christchurch, 2014.

Wilson, Helen, *My First Eighty Years*, Paul's Book Arcade, Hamilton, 1950.